100

THINGS TO DO IN

ASHEVILLE

BEFORE YOU

DIE

Asheville Skyline
Photo courtesy of ExploreAsheville.com

100

THINGS TO DO IN
ASHEVILLE
BEFORE YOU
DIE

KRISTY TOLLEY

REEDY PRESS

Copyright © 2021 by Reedy Press, LLC
Reedy Press
PO Box 5131
St. Louis, MO 63139, USA
www.reedypress.com

Library of Congress Control Number: 2020922400

ISBN: 9781681062952

Design by Jill Halpin

Cover image: Courtesy of ExploreAsheville.com

Printed in the United States of America
21 22 23 24 25 5 4 3 2 1

DEDICATION

For Mom

Turo
Photo courtesy of Old Europe Pastries

CONTENTS

Acknowledgments. xiii

Preface. xiv

Food and Drink

1. Chow Down at Chow Chow: An Asheville Culinary Event 2

2. Nosh Through Asheville on a Food Tour. 4

3. Cure What Ails You at Sovereign Remedies. 6

4. Have a Tea Party at the Inn on Biltmore Estate. 7

5. Lasso an Epic Meal at Farm Burger. 8

6. Sharpen Your Kitchen Skills at Cottage Cooking Asheville 9

7. Sample a Flight at Plēb Urban Winery 10

8. Enjoy Late-Night Date-Night Sweets with Your Sweet
    at Old Europe Pastries 12

9. Search for Your Supper with No Taste Like Home 13

10. Rooftop Hop for Views, Drinks, and History with
    Asheville Rooftop Bar Tours 14

11. Visit Cuba Without a Passport at Hemingway's Cuba. 15

12. Indulge Your Sweet Tooth at French Broad Chocolate Lounge. . . . 16

13. Transport to the Middle East at Jerusalem Garden Café 17

14. Eat Like a Food Show Host 18

15. Taste the Caribbean at Nine Mile Asheville 20

16. Track Down Food Trucks on the Go 21

17. Get in the Spirit of Things at a Distillery. 22

• •

18. Toast to Asheville's First Brewery at Highland Brewing 24

19. Eat BBQ and Take a Selfie at 12 Bones Smokehouse 26

20. Rub Elbows with James Beard Royalty 28

21. Sip a Shake at the Soda Fountain at Woolworth Walk 30

22. Feast on Local Fare (and More) at a Farmers Market 31

23. Pop In for a Pie at Baked Pie Company 34

24. Take the Bus for a Cup of Joe at Double D's Coffee & Desserts 36

25. Brunch with a Beermosa at Lion & Rose Bed and Breakfast 37

26. Go Vegan for a Meal (or Three!) 38

27. Pick a Picnic Spot and Graze 42

Music and Entertainment

28. Map Out Your Visit at the Visitor Center 46

29. Mosey into the World of Moog 47

30. Hit the Trail for Urban Art 48

31. Get Your Art Fix at Museums and Galleries 50

32. Explore Historic Grovewood Village 51

33. Soak in the Busking Scene 52

34. Push Your Boundaries at the Asheville Fringe Arts Festival 53

35. March to the Beat of Your Own Drum in Pritchard Park 54

36. See Asheville in the Movies 55

37. Support Local Artists at the Folk Art Center 56

38. Go with the Flow in the River Arts District 57

39. Catch a Show at Grey Eagle Music Hall 58

40. Lay Down a Track at American Vinyl Co. 59

• •

41. Meet a Motley Fool with Montford Park Players. 60

42. Hop on the Gray Line Trolley 62

43. Ring In the Holidays at the Omni Grove Park Inn
National Gingerbread House Competition. 63

✓ **44.** Walk Along Wall Street 64

✓ **45.** Rove Around Historic Grove Arcade. 66

46. See Clearly at Lexington Glassworks 68

47. Zoom Around the City in a Purple Bus 69

48. Grab a Seat at Silver River Chairs 70

49. Get into the Swing of Things at Empyrean Arts 71

50. Stay Up Late for Nightlife 72

51. Nerd Out at the Asheville Museum of Science 73

Sports and Recreation

52. Cheer on Runners at the Asheville Marathon 76

53. Take Yourself Out to the Ballgame at McCormick Field 77

54. Be a Pinball Wizard at the Asheville Pinball Museum 78

55. Don't Stop Your Bellyaking. 79

56. Get Salty at the Asheville Salt Cave 80

57. Talk to the Animals at Animal Haven of Asheville 82

58. Float Down the French Broad 83

59. Get Spooked on a Ghost Tour with Haunted Asheville. 84

60. Tee Off with a Round of Golf 85

61. Go to the Dogs 86

62. Go Ghost Hunting Along Helen's Bridge 88

• •

63. Amp Up Your Camping with Asheville Glamping 89

64. Stay in a Gem and Sleep Like a King 90

65. Get Lost in Nature at the N.C. Arboretum. 92

66. Stop and Smell the Flowers at the Botanical Gardens. 94

67. Find Your Center in the Mountains 95

68. Peep the Changing Mountain Leaves. 96

69. Explore Asheville's Wild Side at the WNC Nature Center 97

70. Take a Walk in the Woods 98

71. Admire Street Art at Foundation Walls 100

72. Play with Birds of Prey at Curtis Wright Outfitters. 101

Culture and History

73. Be Awed by the St. Lawrence Basilica 104

74. Be Inspired at Burton Street Community Peace Gardens 105

75. Step Back in Time at the Smith-McDowell House Museum. 106

76. Hunt for Historical Gravestones at Riverside Cemetery 107

77. Tune In at the Asheville Radio Museum .108

78. Look Homeward at the Thomas Wolfe Memorial. 109

79. Seek Out a Hidden Castle 110

80. Get a Bird's-Eye View from Biltmore Estate. 111

81. Stroll through History and Art on the Urban Trail 112

82. Channel Your Inner Novelist in the F. Scott Fitzgerald Room 113

83. Get a Glimpse of Art Deco 114

Shopping and Fashion

84. While Away Some Time at Whist 118

85. Shut the Front Door for Home Decor at the Screen Door 119

86. Corral a Deal at the Antique Tobacco Barn. 120

87. Make a Statement at Vintage Moon Modern. 121

88. Hit the Books at a Bookstore 122

89. Find It at Lost and Found. 124

90. Shop 'til You Drop at the Outlets 125

91. Get Your Health On at the Herbiary 126

92. Find the Perfect Vinyl 127

93. Secure a Local Souvenir at Mountain Merch. 128

94. Get Hippy Dippy at Instant Karma 129

95. Appreciate Heritage Arts at the Appalachian Craft Center 130

96. Be Impressed with Kress Emporium 131

97. Buzz Around Asheville Bee Charmer 132

98. Buy Your Basics and More at Mast General Store 133

99. Spice Things Up at the Pepper Palace 134

100. Get Thrifty and Shop Secondhand. 135

Suggested Itineraries 136

Activities by Season 139

Index 141

Great Smoky Mountains National Park
Photo courtesy of iStock

ACKNOWLEDGMENTS

Thanks and gratitude to . . .

Landis Taylor and the entire team at Explore Asheville Convention and Visitors Bureau (ExploreAsheville.com) for answering a million questions as I honed my list.

Dad, Kim, Sloane, Jordan, Wanda, Sarah, Karen, Michele, Janean, Stephanie, Mark, and Raygan for your enthusiasm and support.

Cele and Lynn Seldon for your guidance and encouragement.

Joe, Peyton, and Madden for always being up for a weekend road trip, and for tolerating my incessant need to share every tiny detail of something new I've learned along the way.

• •

PREFACE

On March 10, 2020, I submitted my contract to write *100 Things to Do in Asheville Before You Die*. Little did I know that in just a few short days, a global pandemic would press the pause button on life and travel as we know it.

I've been a frequent visitor to Asheville for over 28 years—ever since my husband and I spent our first anniversary exploring Biltmore Estate and the many other charms Asheville possesses. I already had a long list of Asheville lures I wanted to share in this book. However, being unable to visit this special place for four months was incredibly tough. Eventually, travel restrictions loosened, and the city was able to once again welcome visitors. Although the way we experience Asheville looks a little different now, some things haven't changed. You'll still feel the city's strong sense of community and welcoming spirit. Artists and makers still create beautiful and unique works of art all over Asheville. Award-winning chefs continue to provide innovative dishes. Mountain trails still offer fresh air and awe-inspiring views for those who crave outdoor time.

Asheville brims with iconic attractions, "only here" experiences, and tons of captivating and fun things to do. Within this book, I'll share historical sites, distinct dining opportunities, AAA Four Diamond gems, shopping favorites, and many other things to explore. Whether you're visiting Asheville for the

• •

first time or 50th time, I hope you consider this your guide to discovering the places you didn't know about. It's also my hope that this book inspires you to seek out the family-owned and small businesses—the local makers, doers, and historians that make this eclectic mountain town the beauty she is.

You'll find suggested itineraries in the back of the book, as well as things to do based on the season of your visit. Share your Asheville experience with me on Instagram by using #100ThingsAsheville and let me know what your favorites are!

Biscuit Head
Photo courtesy of Tim Robinson

FOOD AND DRINK

CHOW DOWN
AT CHOW CHOW:
AN ASHEVILLE CULINARY EVENT

This festival is an ideal way to experience the full spectrum of Asheville's culinary scene. Held in September, Chow Chow runs from Friday through Sunday. The idea for the festival was spearheaded by James Beard Award-winning chef Katie Button and French Broad Chocolate's co-founder and CEO, Jael Rattigan. Unlike many food festivals, Chow Chow celebrates the farmers, chefs and makers who are behind the meals and menus that make Asheville such a thriving culinary destination. The diverse flavors of Southern Appalachia are showcased in every event. Festival highlights include behind-the-scenes tastings, tours, farm and chef dinners, hands-on classes, and live music.

(828) 335-8903
chowchowavl.com

OTHER TASTY WAYS TO CHOW DOWN AND QUENCH YOUR THIRST IN ASHEVILLE

Carolina Small Batch Beer Festival
(March)
hiwirebrewing.com
(828) 738-2448

Beer City Week
(May)
avlbeerweek.com

Spring Herb Festival
(May)
(828) 301-8968

Hola Asheville Festival
(June)
(828) 989-2745
holacommunityarts.org

Asheville VeganFest
(October)
(984) 233-6313
ashevilleveganfest.com

Carolina Mountain Cheese Fest
(October)
(828) 484-1586
mountaincheesefest.com

NOSH
THROUGH ASHEVILLE
ON A FOOD TOUR

Asheville is one of the country's hottest culinary destinations. The city snagged the number-one spot on Yelp's list of Top US Foodie Destinations for 2020. Visitors can sample hundreds of breweries, as well as award-winning restaurants. From gourmet international cuisine to home-honed recipes handed down for generations, there's something for every palate. A local food tour is an ideal way to explore them all. Eating Asheville Tours was founded in 2011 by local foodie Stephen Steidle. Three tours are offered—Classic, High Roller, and The Cold One (food and brewery)—and each includes six or seven stops. There's a tour every day of the week with Asheville Food Tours, including the Asheville International Tour, which is also offered as a bilingual tour. Taste Carolina's Asheville Downtown Eats & Drinks Tour showcases a sampling of bites and beverages from local restaurants, bars, and gourmet food stores.

TIP

Come hungry! Food tours provide a generous sampling of Asheville, and you'll be happily sated. If you plan to drink alcohol, always designate a driver.

HERE'S WHERE TO FIND A FOOD TOUR

Eating Asheville
(828) 489-3266
eatingasheville.com

Asheville Food Tours
(828) 243-7401
ashevillefoodtours.com

Taste Carolina
(919) 237-2254
tastecarolina.net

CURE WHAT AILS YOU
AT SOVEREIGN REMEDIES

Located in the building that was once office space for dentists, doctors, barbers, and pharmacists, Sovereign Remedies serves up vegetable-focused fare with a cozy old-school vibe. Their name pays homage to the rich history of herbal medicines many Appalachian families created due to their limited access to traditional forms of medicine. Floor-to-ceiling windows flood the dining room with natural light that seems to showcase the vintage service pieces, gold-framed mirrors, custom-built stools, and other special design touches. Cleverly conceived cocktails are rotated seasonally, but might include the root daiquiri, made with aged rum, sarsaparilla, dandelion, burdock, Demerara, and lime. Thanks to a close relationship with local farmers and purveyors, offerings on their lunch, dinner, and brunch menus may change weekly—think fresh local vegetables crudité, Joyce Farms fried chicken, or hydroponic greens salad.

29 N Market St., (828) 919-9518
sovereignremedies.com

TIP
Bartenders can create a cocktail for you on the fly based on your preferences. Cheers!

HAVE A TEA PARTY
AT THE INN ON BILTMORE ESTATE

Channel your fancy side in true Vanderbilt fashion with afternoon tea. The Vanderbilts often shared this tradition with guests. Sometimes it was a more casual affair with family in the rustic Buck Springs Lodge or by the fire in the Tapestry Gallery. On other occasions, the Vanderbilts hosted more formal tea parties and made use of crisp white tablecloths, sparkling crystal, and their finest tea services—including a Sevres tea service made in France in the early 1800s. During your tea time, you can sample finger sandwiches, sweet and savory canapes, and gourmet cheeses. Choose from an extensive selection of teas like Coco Chai, White Lotus, Assam Gold Leaf, and others. Pinkies up!

One Lodge St., (828) 225-1699
biltmore.com

LASSO AN EPIC MEAL
AT FARM BURGER

They tout themselves as serving up the "best burger in Asheville." It's a lofty claim that they can back up 100 percent. I've dined there as an omnivore, and later as a vegan, and still believe it to be the best burger I've ever had. Their burgers are made from 100 percent grass-fed beef—free of antibiotics, GMOs, and hormones—sourced locally from Hickory Nut Gap Farm. The house-made vegan burger is on point, too. It's made with quinoa, sweet potatoes, roasted mushrooms, kale, and spices, and topped with vegan mayo. Sides like fries (offered four ways), onion rings, and slow-cooked collards round out your meal. Want something lighter? Nosh on the superfood salad, comprised of lacinato kale, shaved red cabbage, hemp seeds, herbs, and crispy black-eyed peas dressed with a grainy mustard vinaigrette. Though it may be a challenge, try and save room for a shake or root beer float.

10 Patton Ave., (828) 348-8540
1831 Hendersonville Rd., (828) 575-2393
farmburger.com

SHARPEN YOUR KITCHEN SKILLS
AT COTTAGE COOKING ASHEVILLE

Ready to elevate your culinary know-how? Sign up for a dinner party-style cooking class with Cottage Cooking. Whether you want to hone your baking skills (A Baker's Dream) or create a delicious, globally inspired menu (A Taste of Thai, The Magic of India, and others), you'll glean a lot from hosts and co-founders John Godts and Liisa Andreassen. In addition to preparing your dish, you'll learn interesting facts and history relating to the meal you create. Vegan and vegetarian classes are also offered. Dishes are often created with vegetables from their own garden. They also procure other ingredients locally, using organic whenever possible. Classes are conducted in the couple's renovated 1950s-style cottage. Their well-equipped home kitchen provides an intimate environment for smaller groups. Eat al fresco in the expansive backyard by the firepit or on the spacious deck.

40 Barnard Ave., (828) 273-3096 or (828) 777-6800
cottagecookingasheville.com

SAMPLE A FLIGHT
AT PLĒB URBAN WINERY

This innovative winery is definitely not your mother's tasting room—unless your mom is super cool, appreciates sustainability practices and has a business that strives to support local purveyors within the Blue Ridge Mountains. Their name is inspired by the plebeian community of ancient Rome—the farmers, builders, bakers, and craftsmen—who were the backbone of the economy. Grapes are locally sourced within a two-hour radius of Asheville. And you can forget the corks. The wines here are kegged and provided by the glass, in a can, or in growlers, which is in line with their mission to produce environmentally friendly and sustainable wines throughout the entire wine-making process. The atmosphere of the winery is as creative as their approach to wine making. It's aptly located in the River Arts District. The spacious tasting room showcases high ceilings, walls dressed with colorful graffiti art, and industrial furnishings.

289 Lyman St., (828) 774-5062
pleburbanwinery.com

Asheville may be Beer City, USA, but that's no reason to sleep on the city's wine offerings. Here are more wineries and tasting rooms to add to your visit.

Little Switzerland Orchard and Winery
This small family-owned orchard and cidery produces small batch fruit wines, meads, and ciders.
405 Elk Park Dr., (828) 337-4354
littleswitzerlandwinery.com

Metro Wines
You'll find a huge selection of wines to pair with any dish or event. They also offer regular tasting events.
169 Charlotte St., (828) 575-9525
metrowinesasheville.com

Asheville Wine Market
Open since 1993, they carry a varied selection of wines from independent (and often family-run) wineries.
65 Biltmore Ave., (828) 253-0060
ashevillewine.com

Biltmore Estate Winery
Visit the winery on your own or opt for one of their exclusive tours—Behind-the-Scenes Winery Tour and Tasting and Red Wine & Chocolate Tasting.
One Lodge St., (800) 411-3812
biltmore.com/visit/winery

ENJOY LATE-NIGHT DATE-NIGHT SWEETS
WITH YOUR SWEET
AT OLD EUROPE PASTRIES

When Melinda and Zoltan Vetro arrived in the United States from Hungary in 1994, they wasted no time building their American dream. In Hungary, Melinda attended a culinary institute and became a skilled baker. It seemed natural to open a pastry shop and share those gifts with Asheville. For the past 25 years, Old Europe Pastries has served as the perfect late-night date spot for a cup of coffee and a delectable pastry. Zoltan passed away in 2010, but their son Bence continues to assist Melinda with their thriving business. Popular menu items are also some of the most traditional and Hungarian-inspired pastries, like the French Creamy. Best date-night selection? Melinda says tiramisu—light, fluffy layers of cake with alternating layers of a coffee brandy soak, mascarpone cheese mousse, whipped cream, and topped with a light dusting of cocoa powder. How can you not fall in love with that? They've expanded their menu over the years to include delicious gluten-free and vegan options. Melinda believes everyone should have something sweet to eat. I couldn't agree more! They're open until 10 p.m. Monday through Thursday, and until 11 p.m. Friday through Sunday. Whatever your date-night plans entail, make sure they end here!

13 Broadway St., (828) 255-5999
oldeuropepastries.com

SEARCH FOR YOUR SUPPER
WITH NO TASTE LIKE HOME

It began as a side hustle created from a hobby. Like many locals, Alan Muskat often foraged on his own. Living hyper local is a characteristic of Asheville. In 1995, Muskat decided to turn his hobby into a business, picking items for local restaurants and earning money from teaching others how to forage. Classes evolved into tours, and No Taste Like Home was born. Expert guides lead participants on foraging walks that include a brief cooking lesson and tasting. You'll also get a free appetizer with lunch, brunch, or dinner at a local restaurant. Tours like the Wild Food Stroll and No Taste Like Home are offered through the spring, summer, and fall. When COVID-19 sequestered folks at home, another tour was added: What's in My Yard? A guide leads you through your yard and identifies edibles you likely never knew were there.

(828) 209-8599
notastelikehome.org

ROOFTOP HOP FOR VIEWS, DRINKS, AND HISTORY
WITH ASHEVILLE ROOFTOP BAR TOURS

Few activities are more relaxing than enjoying a cocktail while you soak in sweeping sunset views of the landscape below. Add a couple more rooftops and pepper in a little local history, and you have a memorable and Instagram-worthy evening with friends. Each tour with Asheville Rooftop Bar Tours includes three stops at some of the city's best rooftop restaurants and bars. While you sip, your guide opens a window to the past, sharing historical 19th-century and early 20th-century photos of bygone Asheville cityscapes. Cozy firepits and outdoor heaters mean you can hop on a tour any time of the year. Choose from The Rooftop Sunset Tour, The Sky's the Limit Tour, and The Bird's Eye View Tour. You can also opt for a customized group tour—think bachelorette parties, friends' get-togethers, or family reunions. If you don't drink alcohol (or are the designated driver for the evening), they have you covered! Mocktails are available at each location.

45 S French Broad Ave., Ste. 170, (828) 774-7785
ashevillerooftoopbartours.com

VISIT CUBA WITHOUT A PASSPORT
AT HEMINGWAY'S CUBA

If you weren't able to make it to Cuba when President Obama loosened travel restrictions for Americans, don't fret. Thanks to Tony Fraga, owner of Hemingway's Cuba (and Havana native), you can at least get a taste of it. Fraga had long wanted to open a Cuban restaurant in Asheville, and a return visit to Havana in 2016 spurred his vision. He dined at El Floridita, the restaurant at which he often visited as a child with his own father. When Fraga returned to Asheville, he decided the time was right to bring a slice of Cuba to the Asheville community, and opened Hemingway's Cuba the following year. Grab a rooftop table and enjoy panoramic views as you savor dishes like masas de cerdo fritas (crispy Hickory Nut Gap pork with onions and garlic) or an el Cubano sandwich (sweet ham, slow-roasted pork, Swiss cheese, pickles, and mustard). Fraga's son Alex recommends the Ropa Vieja, a slow-braised shredded beef stew with roasted red peppers and olives. "I love the tender beef and the sauce," he shares. "This dish reminds me of family and gatherings, as it's a Cuban favorite." Whatever you decide to order, make sure to add a perfect Hemingway's Daiquiri.

15 Page Ave., (828) 417-6866
hemingwayscuba.com

INDULGE YOUR SWEET TOOTH
AT FRENCH BROAD CHOCOLATE LOUNGE

If you're strolling along Pack Square and notice a line of people stretching out from a charming light blue building with brown trim, march yourself right over and join them. The wait may be long—sometimes 45 minutes or more—but it will be worth every second. French Broad Chocolate Lounge has received accolades from national publications like *Southern Living, Vogue, Food & Wine*, and *Forbes*. And for good reason. Owners (and husband and wife) Dan and Jael Rattigan have been crafting artisan chocolate directly from the source since 2012. Their passion for creating quality chocolate goes back even further. After they married in 2003, they ventured to Costa Rica and opened a dessert shop and café. Three years later, they settled in Asheville and began making chocolate out of their home kitchen, selling at local farmers markets and online. Demand grew quickly, and the French Broad Chocolate Lounge opened in 2008. It might be hard to choose from the selection of delectable bars, bonbons, brownies, cakes, cookies, and ice cream. They have plenty of vegan and gluten-free goodies, too. Want to see how the magic happens? Check out the 14,000-square-foot Chocolate Factory and Café, which offers tours daily.

Chocolate Lounge: 10 South Pack Square, (828) 252-4181
Chocolate Factory: 821 Riverside Dr., (828) 348-5187
frenchbroadchocolates.com

08/21/21 w/ Julie.
Very Good.

TRANSPORT TO THE MIDDLE EAST
AT JERUSALEM GARDEN CAFÉ

When Jerusalem Garden Café opened in 1993, there were very few restaurants in Asheville serving international cuisine. The recipes for many menu items were passed on to owner Farouk Badr from his family in Jordan. Get your fill with freshly prepared hummus, couscous, falafel wraps, lamb kabobs, shawarma, and more. A meal here is more than a plate of flavorful and authentic Mediterranean and Middle Eastern dishes, though. It's a dining experience that transports you to an exotic place—one that allows diners to savor not only the food, but the culture as well. Brightly hued tents imported from Egypt drape from the ceiling. On Friday and Saturday nights, diners are treated with belly dancing performances accompanied by live music. Weekends are popular nights to dine, so make sure and reserve your table in advance.

79 Patton Ave., (828) 254-0255
jerusalemgardencafe.com

TIP
Make a reservation to dine in the "tent room," where you can opt to eat at one of the floor tables. It's located at the far end of the main dining area. The walls are lined with colorful fabric, creating a mini retreat fit for a king.

EAT
LIKE A FOOD SHOW HOST

Have you ever found yourself binging on food channel shows thinking how cool it would be to have a job like that? A visit to Asheville can provide a sampling of that tasty life. The city's thriving culinary scene makes it a natural lure for the Travel Channel, Food Network, and the Cooking Channel. Just last year, Asheville's own Reza Setayesh, owner and chef of BimBeriBon, came out on top during his battle on an episode of *Beat Bobby Flay*. The Travel Channel's *Food Paradise* showcased Biscuit Head, Asheville Sandwich Co., Early Girl Eatery, 12 Bones, and Rocky's Hot Chicken Shack on various episodes over the years. Twelve Bones and Biscuit Head also made an appearance in Food Network shows, along with Rhubarb, Chai Pani, Moose Café, and Buxton Hall. Luella's Bar-B-Que, The Blackbird, and Cucina 24 have made appearances on the Cooking Channel. I think it's safe to say that the above list will only get longer over time!

ADD THESE SPOTS TO YOUR FOOD HOST ITINERARY

BimBeriBon
697 Haywood Rd.,
(828) 505-0328
bimberibon.com

Biscuit Head
733 Haywood Rd.,
(828) 333-5145
417 Biltmore Ave.,
(828) 505-3449
1994 Hendersonville Rd.,
(828) 585-2055
biscuitheads.com

Asheville Sandwich Co.
794 Haywood Rd.,
(828) 505-8070
ashevillesandwich
company.com

Early Girl Eatery
8 Wall St., (828) 259-9292
444 Haywood Rd., #101,
(828) 820-2323
earlygirleatery.com

12 Bones
5 Foundy St., Ste. 10,
(828) 253-4499
12bones.com

Rocky's Hot Chicken Shack
1455 Patton Ave.,
(828) 575-2260
rockyshotchickenshack.com

Rhubarb
7 SW Pack Square,
(828) 785-1503
rhubarbasheville.com

Chai Pani
22 Battery Park Ave.,
(828) 254-4003
chaipaniasheville.com

Moose Café
570 Brevard Rd.,
(828) 255-0920
eatatthemoosecafe.com

Buxton Hall
32 Banks Ave.,
(828) 232-7216
buxtonhall.com

Luella's Bar-B-Que
501 Merrimon Ave.,
(828) 505-7427
33 Town Square Blvd.,
(828) 676-3855
luellasbbq.com

The Blackbird
47 Biltmore Ave.,
(828) 254-2502
theblackbirdrestaurant.com

Cucina 24
24 Wall St., (828) 254-6170
cucina24restaurant.com

TASTE THE CARIBBEAN
AT NINE MILE ASHEVILLE

If a Jamaican escape eludes you at the moment, a meal here should hold you over until you can get there. The restaurant is named for a district in Jamaica's Saint Ann Parish. Nine Mile was the birthplace and final resting place of reggae musician and peace activist Bob Marley. The menu boasts Caribbean fusion dishes that include a good selection of vegetarian, vegan, and gluten-free options. Start off with an appetizer of Humble Hummus, then tuck into the Irie Ites—chicken or tofu sautéed with white wine and fresh veggies in a rich, dairy-free basil pesto and tossed with cavatappi pasta. Each entrée is served with the ridiculously delicious, locally baked City Bakery Natty bread. Daily specials and frequently changing menu items ensure that no two visits will be identical. Whether you dine at the original location in historic Montford, or opt for the West Asheville or South Asheville restaurants, just get yourself there.

Montford: 233 Montford Ave., (828) 505-3121
South Asheville: One Town Square Blvd., (828) 676-1807
West Asheville: 751 Haywood Rd., (828) 575-9903
ninemileasheville.com

TRACK DOWN FOOD TRUCKS
ON THE GO

The fleet of food trucks in Asheville is almost limitless. From vegetarian and vegan to BBQ and comfort food (and everything in between), there's a mobile meal around to satisfy every palate. You can find them at special events like the Asheville Food Truck Festival or hit them up at the WNC Agricultural Center, local breweries, and other spots. The best way to find your favorites is to go online. Thanks to ashevillefoodtrucks.com, you don't have to Google endlessly to find them all. Here you can peruse a full food truck list, as well as a comprehensive list of local breweries—I mean, it is sort of the perfect marriage. Don't miss: Root Down (Creole-inspired Southern soul food), Melt Your Heart (gourmet grilled cheese and specialty sandwiches), and Appalachian Chic (Southern fusion farm-to-fork).

Root Down, (828) 808-5312
rootdownfoodtruck.com

Melt Your Heart, (828) 989-6749
facebook.com/Melt-Your-Heart-193294404119434

Appalachian Chic, (828) 782-8484
facebook.com/appchicfoodtruck

GET IN THE SPIRIT
OF THINGS AT A DISTILLERY

North Carolina was the first Southern state to enact Prohibition, fueling bootleggers to pursue financial opportunities with their own brews. Corn was plentiful in Southern Appalachia, and the Scots-Irish who settled there brought their distillation methods with them, making good use of it. Thankfully, Prohibition is long gone, and we can freely imbibe at locally owned distilleries. Dalton Distillery, the first legal distillery in downtown Asheville, has been a local favorite since 2010. They were also the first in the state to produce and sell their own spirits. They do it all from scratch—down to building their own pot stills. Their Hammond Rum is crafted in the Caribbean style, and made with a blend of four types of sugars. Other flavors include Appleachian (made with crushed Blue Ridge-grown apples), Hammond Coffee Flavored Rum (using their own homemade coffee extract), Hammond Oak Rum, and Arana Blanca Vodka. Gin lovers should make a beeline to The Chemist. This women-owned, small batch gin distillery snagged both "Distillery of the Year" and "Mixologist of the Year" at the North Carolina Restaurant & Lodging Association's Chef Showdown just under two years of being open. Enjoy a drink at Chemist Spirits' three-floor 19th-century lounge, Antidote. In addition to signature and classic cocktails, you can choose something from their craft beer or European wine menu.

Dalton Distillery
251 Biltmore Ave., (828) 785-1499
dalton-distillery.com

The Chemist
151 Coxe Ave., (828) 263-6943
chemistspirits.com

There are more places in Asheville to raise a toast to the end of Prohibition. Here are additional places to enjoy unique spirits, tours, and tastings:

Asheville Distilling Co.
Heirloom corn purchased from local farmers might be the secret sauce to their handcrafted whiskeys. One variety of heirloom white corn used in T&S Platinum (the first premium American moonshine) only grows in the region's mountain valleys.

12 Old Charlotte Hwy., Ste. 140, (828) 575-2000
ashevilledistilling.com

Cultivated Cocktails Distillery
Formerly H&H Distillery, they provide a small batch-made spirit for every type of drinker—whiskey, rum, gin, vodka, and coffee liquor. Enjoy a craft cocktail (or two), and buy a few bar goods or mixers while you're there.

29 Page Ave., (828) 338-9779
cultivated-cocktails.com

Eda Rhyne Distilling Company
Many of the botanicals used in their spirits are harvested locally—some from owner Rett Murphy's own farm, and some foraged from the surrounding mountains. Their Amaro Flora, Appalachian Fernet, and Rustic Nocino are interpretations of generations-old regional medicinals.

101 Fairview Rd., Ste. A, (828) 412-5441
edarhyne.com

TOAST TO ASHEVILLE'S FIRST BREWERY
AT HIGHLAND BREWING

Raise a pint to Oscar Wong, the retired engineer who opened Highland Brewing in 1994—the city's first brewery since Prohibition. It began as a small 12,000-square-foot brewery situated in the basement of a downtown pizza restaurant. The brewery was built mostly with retrofitted dairy equipment. Today, patrons have plenty of room to spread out in the spacious taproom on Old Charlotte Highway and quench their thirst with year-round staples like Gaelic Ale (their original brew) and Daycation IPA (light with herbal notes and hints of citrus), or seasonal selections like Midnight Summit (think creamy vanilla with a touch of coffee and chocolate) and Thunderstruck (brewed with one-and-a-half pounds of locally produced coffee). Returning to their roots, Highland Brewing opened an additional taproom in downtown's historic S&W Building, home of a popular chef-curated food hall.

12 Old Charlotte Hwy., (828) 299-3370
highlandbrewing.com

Highland Brewery started Asheville's beer revolution. With nearly 40 breweries, the city is consistently ranked as one of the leading destinations for craft beer. Here are some top spots:

Asheville Brewing Company

Whether you want to take in a $3 movie, nosh on seriously good pizza and pub fare, or have a side of Bloody Mary with your craft beer, you're covered.

77 Coxe Ave., (828) 255-4077
675 Merrimon Ave., (828) 254-1281
1850 Hendersonville Rd., Ste. A, (828) 277-5775
ashevillebrewing.com

Green Man Brewery

One of Asheville's oldest breweries (1997), this European-style brewery serves up fresh hop-forward beers at two locations: the three-story Green Mansion and Dirty Jack's.

27 Buxton Ave. and 15 Buxton Ave., (828) 252-5502
greenmanbrewery.com

Burial Beer Co.

Its industrial yet cozy taproom is a popular spot for beer lovers, offering favorites like Bolo Coconut Brown Ale and the Skillet Donut Stout. Grab a light bite or a big main from the brewery's restaurant, Salt & Smoke. The menu changes regularly. You can't leave before you've had your picture taken in front of the mural of Tom Selleck and Sloth from *The Goonies*.

40 Collier Ave., (828) 475-2739
10 Shady Oak Dr., (828) 505-4452
burialbeer.com

Thirsty Monk Brewery

They operate a family of brewpubs in the city, as well as in Denver, Colorado, and Portland, Oregon. The downtown brewery has two floors. Upstairs in the Craft Bar, they offer a solid variety of American craft beers. The basement houses the Belgian Bar, which features a good selection of imported brews. Pair your pint with one of their scratch-made pies (roasted vegetables, steak and cheese, and more).

90 Patton Ave., (828) 254-5470
2 Town Square Blvd., #170, (828) 687-3873
monkpub.com

EAT BBQ
AND TAKE A SELFIE
AT 12 BONES SMOKEHOUSE

Who doesn't love to share photos of their dinner out on Instagram? There's plenty to feed you and your feed at 12 Bones. I mean, if President Obama declared 12 Bones to be the second reason for coming back to Asheville, you know it's good. (The people here topped his list.) All their meats are slow smoked to tender perfection. Choose from chicken, turkey, pulled pork, and brisket. Top it with one of their creative barbecue sauces like Pineapple Habanero or Blueberry Chipotle. Round out your meal with scratch-made sides like jalapeno cheese grits, mac and cheese, collard greens, and their "damn good corn puddin'." When you're finished, wipe the sauce off your mouth and take a selfie! Twelve Bones is located at the Foundation, a 13-acre complex of repurposed buildings covered in street art (the only place in Asheville where street art is legal). The walls make for a fun and funky backdrop for your photo op.

5 Foundy St., Ste. 10, (828) 253-4499
12bones.com

Truth be told, there are a slew of great barbecue spots in Asheville, and you can't go wrong with any of them. Here are a few favorites from which to choose.

Little Pigs BBQ
384 McDowell St., (828) 254-4253
littlepigsbbq.net

Buxton Hall Barbecue
32 Banks Ave., (828) 232-7216
buxtonhall.com

Bonfire BBQ & Catering
1056 Patton Ave., (828) 255-0020
bonfireavl.com

Moe's Original BBQ
4 Sweeten Creek Rd., #1, (828) 505-8282
moesoriginalbbq.com

Luella's Bar-B-Que
501 Merrimon Ave., (828) 505-7427
luellasbbq.com

Black Bear BBQ
800 Fairview Rd., Ste. C8, (828) 298-1035
blackbearbbqavl.com

Dickey's Barbecue Pit
1636 Hendersonville Rd., Ste. 125, (828) 277-5221
dickeys.com

Shortie's Drive-Thru BBQ
6 Newfound Rd., (828) 505-7824
shortiesbbq.com

RUB ELBOWS
WITH JAMES BEARD ROYALTY

James Beard was arguably one of the most influential people in the culinary world. He hosted the first-ever cooking program in 1946, paving the way for today's celebrity chefs. The James Beard Foundation Awards honor chefs, bakers, restaurants, bar programs, and others who continue to incite change in the food and beverage industry. Earning a James Beard Award is sort of a chef's Oscar equivalent. Asheville's vibrant food scene makes it one of the South's most eclectic and exciting food cities, and James Beard Award-winning chefs are in no short supply here. Chef Katie Button of Curaté Tapas Bar and La Bodega by Curaté has several under her apron strings—semifinalist for the James Beard Rising Star Chef award, semifinalist for Best Chefs in America, and nominee for Best Chef Southeast, among several others. Meherwan Irani, chef and owner of Chai Pani, has earned several nominations for Best Chef in the Southeast. Other award-winning chefs include Jacob Sessoms, Table; Ashleigh Shanti, Benne on Eagle; Elliott Moss, Buxton Hall Barbecue; John Fleer, Rhubarb; and Brian Canipelli, Cucina 24.

WHERE TO FIND
JAMES BEARD ROYALTY

Curaté
13 Biltmore Ave., (828) 239-2946
La Bodega by Curaté
32 S Lexington Ave., (828) 630-0330
katiebuttonrestaurants.com

Chai Pani
22 Battery Park Ave., (828) 254-4003
chaipaniasheville.com

Table
48 College St., (828) 254-8980
tableasheville.com

Benne on Eagle
35 Eagle St., (828) 552-8833
benneoneagle.com

Buxton Hall Barbecue
32 Banks Ave., (828) 232-7216
buxtonhall.com

Rhubarb
7 SW, N Pack Square, (828) 785-1503
rhubarbasheville.com

Cucina 24
24 Wall St., (828) 254-6170
cucina24restaurant.com

SIP A SHAKE
AT THE SODA FOUNTAIN
AT WOOLWORTH WALK

Wax nostalgia with a treat from one of the city's historic landmarks. Situated in the original 1938 F.W. Woolworth building, the Soda Fountain was built to mirror the original Woolworth Luncheonette—bright red seating and chrome finishes throughout. The menu features delicious deli sandwiches like thick-sliced fried bologna, chicken salad, and Woolworth's BLT. They also serve hotdogs, burgers, and salads, as well as many original items such as egg creams and old-fashioned ice cream sodas. After your meal, check out Woolworth Walk's spacious gallery, which showcases the work of over 150 local artisans. It's Asheville's largest exclusively local artist gallery.

25 Haywood St., (828) 254-9210
woolworthwalk.com

FEAST ON LOCAL FARE (AND MORE)
AT A FARMERS MARKET

For many people, a visit to the farmers market (or tailgate market) each weekend is tradition. What's better than feasting on vine-ripe heirloom tomatoes, homegrown cucumbers, and juicy peaches in the summertime? There's also something about relying on your local farmers and makers for your food and sundries that creates a deeper connection to your community. Stretched on a 36-acre site, WNC Farmers Market teems with everything from fresh produce, local honey, mixes, and meats to arts and crafts, soaps, souvenirs, and baked goods. It's open every day with a bounty of seasonal goodies. There are several buildings, including two huge wholesale buildings and five open-air truck sheds that can accommodate 194 farmers. There's also the Jesse Israel & Sons Garden Center—probably the best around. They're family-owned and offer an extensive selection of herbs, house plants, trees, landscape plants, and garden supplies. They also offer a seasonal Christmas shop complete with unique ornaments and varied holiday decorations. Take a break and grab a bite at Moose's—farm-to-fork meals and exceptional mountain views.

WNC Farmers Market
570 Brevard Rd., (828) 253-1691
facebook.com/wncfarmersmarket

Although it's the largest, WNC Farmers Market isn't the only place to feast on local fare in Asheville. Grab your reusable bags or a basket and check out these other markets.

North Asheville Tailgate Market
Head to the picturesque campus of UNC Asheville for Western North Carolina's oldest producer-only farmers market. Operating since 1980, this market takes place from 8 a.m. to noon every Saturday. Peruse more than 70 vendors' stands that offer a bevy of produce, locally made bakery items, dairy products, jewelry, pottery, and more.

3300 University Heights, (828) 484-6296
northashevilletailgatemarket.com

River Arts District Farmers Market
Held at Plēb Urban Winery each Wednesday from 3 to 6 p.m., this producer-only market has it all. Stock up on fresh flowers and herbs, baked goods and artisan foods, a bounty of garden-grown vegetables, and meats. You'll also find specialty items like candles, soaps, salves, and medicinal herbs. Relax with a flight of wine at Plēb or fill up your growler before you head home. An indoor market takes place during the winter months.

289 Lyman St. (at Plēb Urban Winery),
(828) 774-5062
radfarmersmarket.com

East Asheville Tailgate Market
Pop by Groce United Methodist Church every Friday, May through October. From 3 to 6 p.m., an eclectic lineup of full-time and part-time vendors showcases baked goods, seafood, fruits and vegetables, pottery, and a variety of other offerings. Mark off your gift list during their Holiday Market that takes place on a Saturday in mid-December.

954 Tunnel Rd., (828) 458-2270
eastashevillemarket.com

West Asheville Tailgate Market
Beginning early April, this market takes place on Tuesdays from 3:30 to 6:30 p.m., through late November. It's located in the Grace Baptist Church parking lot. Peruse an abundant variety of local produce, cheeses, meat, and poultry, as well as specialty goods like herbal medicines, natural beauty products, and locally made art. Enjoy live music as you shop. If you're shopping with young ones, check out the free activities at the kids' booth.

718 Haywood Rd.
westashevilletailgatemarket.com

POP IN FOR A PIE
AT BAKED PIE COMPANY

After a day of shopping during the summer of 2016, Kirsten Fuchs and her daughter decided to cap off the day with a piece of pie and a cup of coffee. The problem? They couldn't find a place to go. That's when the oven light went on in Kirsten's mind, and Baked Pie Company was open the following year. It didn't take long for the idea to catch on, and a second location was added within seven months of the first one. The list of baked and cream pie flavors changes daily, though honey pecan and brownie fudge pies are permanent fixtures on the menu. Each day, they choose about 15 pies from more than 100 recipes they rotate. The menu always includes vegan, gluten-free, sugar-free, and keto options. Can't decide which pie to order? No worries! Go for a pie flight of any three flavors. (The idea came to Kirsten during a dinner out one night that included a beer flight.) If you'd prefer a pie all to yourself, give them 48-hour notice, and they'll hook you up.

South Asheville
4 Long Shoals Rd., (828) 333-4366

North Asheville
50 N Merrimon Ave., (828) 210-9544
bakedpiecompany.com

SATISFY YOUR SWEET TOOTH AT OTHER AREA BAKERIES

Old World Levain Bakery (aka OWL Bakery)
295 Haywood Rd., (828) 785-1770
owlbakery.com

Karen Donatelli Bakery & Café
57 Haywood St., (828) 225-5751
facebook.com/KarenDonatelliBakeryCafe

Geraldine's
840 Merrimon Ave., (828) 252-9330
geraldinesbakeryavl.com

Amy's Bakery
1400 Cold Stream Ct., #302, (530) 999-8005
facebook.com/amysueeliason

TAKE THE BUS FOR A CUP OF JOE
AT DOUBLE D'S COFFEE & DESSERTS

You might think you've been transported to England when you catch a glimpse of the bright red Londoners' double-decker bus parked along Aston and Biltmore. The 1963 Lodekka model served as transportation in Bristol, England, until the 1970s. After a stint as a party bus in Atlanta, it made its way to Asheville—and became the home of Double D's in 1999. Since then, the bus has been the "go to" spot for coffee and desserts for residents and tourists alike. Their coffees and teas are all locally roasted and organic. Sip on a signature beverage (served hot or cold) like Crème Brue Latte, Lavender Honey Latte, or a Red Hot Chile Mocha. The mouthwatering desserts here—muffins, brownies, and cookies—are Asheville-made, too. Grab a bite to go as you head out for a day's exploration, sit a spell at one of the patio tables, or scoot in a booth on the roof and savor your treat as you survey your kingdom below.

41 Biltmore Ave., (828) 505-2439
doubledscoffee.com

TIP
Bring your bills. It's a cash-only establishment. Stop by and say "hey" to the bus driver and his dog, though they likely won't respond—they're a little "stiff."

BRUNCH WITH A BEERMOSA
AT LION & ROSE BED AND BREAKFAST

Situated within Asheville's Montford Historic District, this charming Queen Anne-style bed-and-breakfast dates back to 1898. Guests are often impressed with the fireplaces in some of the rooms, original features like stained-glass windows, and antique or period-style furnishings. But it's the unique and totally Asheville way of welcoming guests that will have you booking your next stay before you leave—a cold pint of home-brewed beer, made right on the premises. Innkeepers Karen and Steve Wilson had been brewing their own beer for about five years and decided to offer it to guests. It's been such a hit, they strive to have one or two kegs available at all times to accommodate them. Often, guests will offer feedback and suggestions on their favorites, which ensures the popular flavors are in rotation. Summer guests are greeted with a more wheat-style beer (or perhaps a beer slushie!), while fall visitors can sample a holiday flavor (think pumpkin spice). As with most bed-and-breakfasts, your morning meal is included here. The difference? Sip on a beermosa with your Sunday brunch. It's a guest favorite—some tasters say they actually prefer it to a traditional mimosa. It pairs remarkably well with their signature orange ricotta pancakes.

276 Montford Ave., (828) 255-7673
lion-rose.com

GO VEGAN
FOR A MEAL (OR THREE!)

With the city's long-established farm-to-table mindset, it's no surprise that the plant-based game here is extremely strong. Whether you're a vegan or vegetarian, or you just want to add more healthy meals to your rotation, Asheville's selection of plant-based restaurants is extensive and delicious. Additionally, many traditional restaurants in Asheville are vegan-friendly—offering plant-based options on their regular menu or allowing substitutions on dishes to accommodate vegan diners.

Located downtown on historic Wall Street, Laughing Seed Café was Asheville's first vegetarian restaurant. It's won a bevy of awards, including being named Best Vegetarian Restaurant in WNC for the past 14 years by *Asheville Citizen Times* and *Mountain Express*. Choose from sandwiches, pizzas, family-style meals, desserts, and specialty cocktails. Whatever you order, make sure you add a side of the vegan queso for your hand-cut sweet potato chips.

Named one of the best vegan restaurants in the country by Zagat, Plant offers innovative and vibrant vegan cuisine in a contemporary setting. Freshly prepared menu items include grilled beets, smoked portobello, and seitan chile con queso. End on a sweet note with a slice of carrot cake or cardamom crème brûlée.

Laughing Seed Café	Plant
40 Wall St., (828) 252-3445	165 Merrimon Ave., (828) 258-7500
laughingseed.com	plantisfood.com

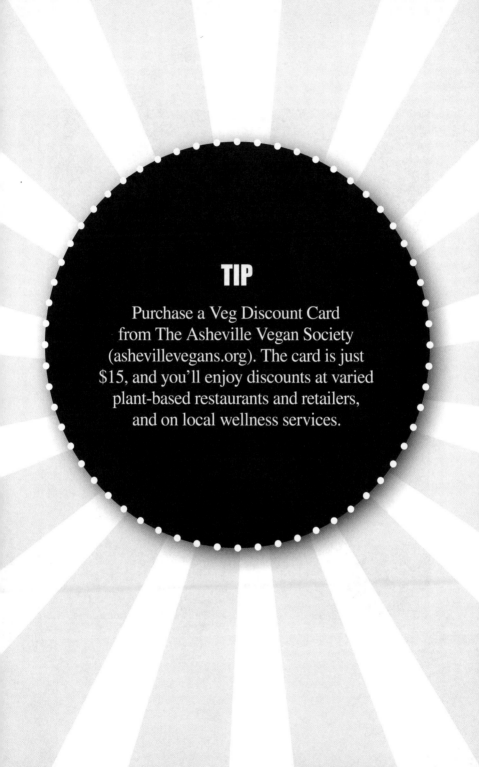

TIP

Purchase a Veg Discount Card
from The Asheville Vegan Society
(ashevillevegans.org). The card is just
$15, and you'll enjoy discounts at varied
plant-based restaurants and retailers,
and on local wellness services.

Venture on for more vegan and vegetarian dining options. Here are a few others to consider:

Sunflower Diner

Nosh on breakfast and lunch items like the North African grits and greens bowl, biscuits and gravy, a mock Philly, or a grilled pimiento cheese.

771 Haywood Rd., (828) 225-4952
westvillagemarket.com/sunflower-diner

Vortex Doughnuts

Weekly rotating eclectic flavors of both non-vegan and vegan doughnuts make it a must-stop for locals and tourists alike. Follow them on social media for the latest selections.

32 Banks Ave., Ste. 106, (828) 552-3010
vortexdoughnuts.com

Rosetta's Kitchen

Get your fill on soul-warming comfort food. All vegetarian (but largely vegan), the menu includes nachos, sandwiches, and the "family favorite"— peanut butter baked tofu, served with sautéed kale and smashed potatoes with gravy.

116 N Lexington Ave., (828) 232-0738
rosettaskitchen.com

Early Girl Eatery

Great for all palates, this spot serves up Southern breakfast foods, fresh sandwiches, and more. The menu features lots of delicious vegan, vegetarian, and gluten-free options.

8 Wall St., (828) 259-9292
earlygirleatery.com

Green Sage Café

Meat eaters and plant-based folks dining together will all be happy here. All food is sustainably sourced, organic, hormone- and antibiotic-free, grass-fed, and crazy good. Breakfast is served all day, too.

5 Broadway St., (828) 252-4450
633 Merrimon Ave., Ste. A, (828) 417-7859
1800 Hendersonville Rd., (828) 274-4450
70 Westgate Pkwy., (828) 785-1780

PICK A PICNIC SPOT
AND GRAZE

A sunny day, clean air, fresh food, and good company—what better way is there to enjoy a meal than picnic style? Create your own basket from your personal pantry, or order a meal to go from your favorite Asheville restaurant. Roman's Deli & Catering and Asheville Sandwich Company are both good bets. Or, you can let The Rhu pack your picnic. Choose from custom meals that include sandwiches, salads, brunch items, cheeses, wines, charcuterie, baked goodies, and other treats, or they'll curate one to your liking. Pack it up with one of their reusable tote bags, or bring your own basket to fill with their fully disposable picnic accessories and serving pieces. Forgot your blanket? Purchase one from The Rhu (along with other reusable camping accoutrements).

Roman's Deli & Catering
75 Haywood St., (828) 505-1552
ieatlocal.com

Asheville Sandwich Company
794 Haywood Rd., (828) 505-8070
ashevillesandwichcompany.com

The Rhu
10 S Lexington Ave., (828) 785-1799
the-rhu.com

TIP
For inspiration and great picnicking tips, grab a copy of Ashley English's book, *A Year of Picnics: Recipes for Dining Well in the Great Outdoors.*

PACK UP AND HEAD TO ONE OF THESE SCENIC SPOTS!

Botanical Gardens at Asheville

More than 600 species native to the Southern Appalachians live here. The gardens are rich in bloom through most of the spring and summer months. Dine among vibrant wildflowers, trees, shrubs, magnolia trees, and other flora.

151 W.T. Weaver Blvd., (828) 252-5190
ashevillebotanicalgardens.org

Biltmore Estate

There's thousands of acres to explore. Within them, you'll find perfect picnic spots like the sloped lawn in front of the marble statue of Diana, around the Bass Lake, or along one of the many nature trails.

One Lodge St., (800) 411-3812
biltmore.com

Craggy Gardens

Located along milepost 364 along the Blue Ridge Parkway, this spot offers stunning views awash with pink and purple blooming rhododendrons and other vibrant floral displays. Take a post-picnic hike along one of the soul-restorative hiking trails.

199 Hemphill Knob Rd., (828) 348-3400
nps.gov/blri/planyourvisit/craggy-gardens.htm

Lake Powhatan Recreation Area

Find this picnic spot within the Bent Creek Experimental Forest. The picnic area includes 22 tables, as well as a swimming beach, hiking and biking trails, and a fishing pier.

375 Wesley Branch Rd., (828) 257-4200
fs.usda.gov/recarea/nfsnc/recarea/?recid=48174

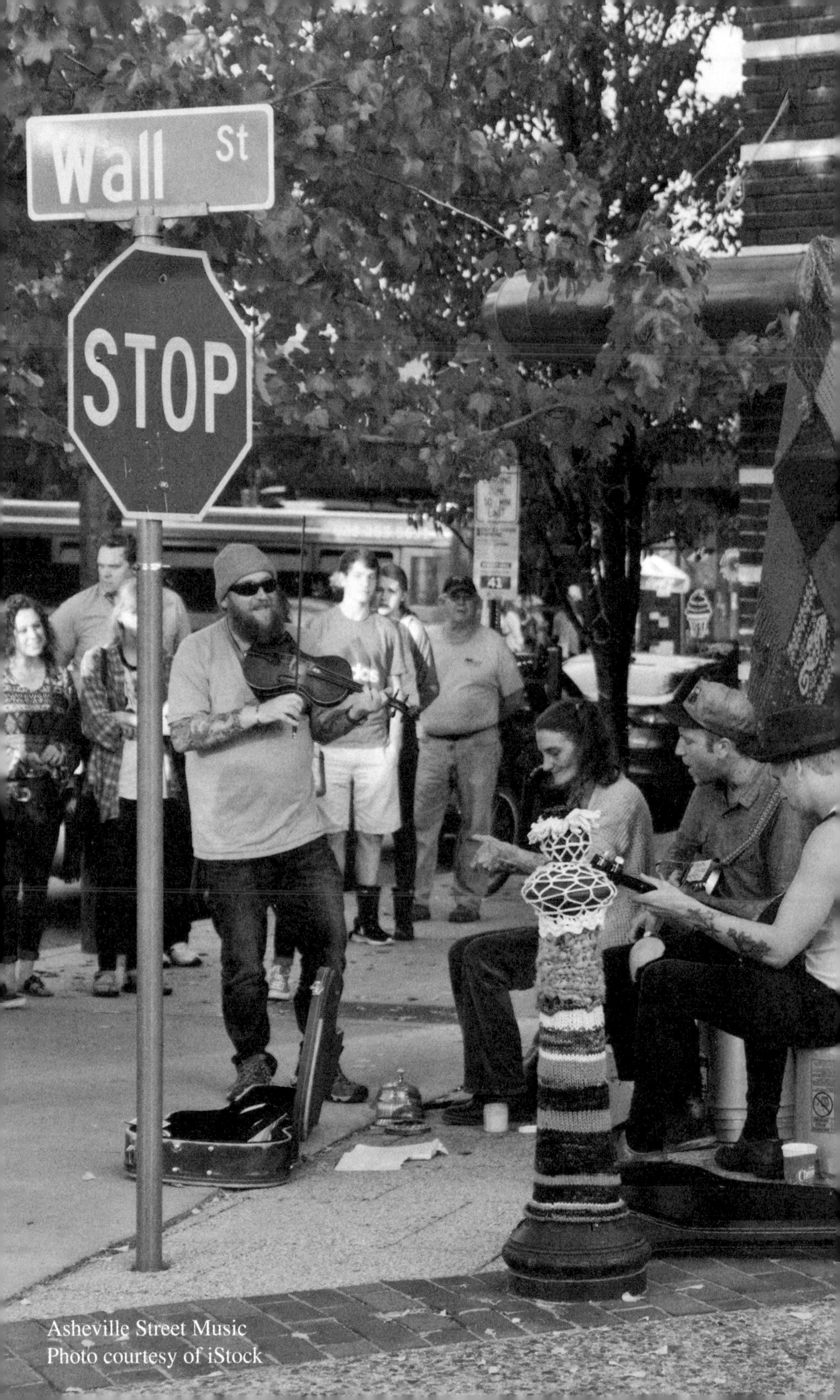

Asheville Street Music
Photo courtesy of iStock

MUSIC AND ENTERTAINMENT

08/21/21 w/ Julie.

MAP OUT YOUR VISIT
AT THE VISITOR CENTER

No matter how many times you visit Asheville, there's always something new to explore. That's why it's a good idea to make the Visitor Center your first stop. You can find out about new restaurants and attractions or discover well-established places you might have missed during previous visits. Plus, they provide attraction coupons and special packages that will help you save money while you're here!

36 Montford Ave., (828) 258-6101
exploreasheville.com

08/21/21 w/ Julie

MOSEY
INTO THE WORLD OF MOOG

You don't have to be a music fanatic to appreciate the impact of Dr. Robert Moog's contribution to the world of music. Historically, synthesizers were humongous (the first ones weighed about 115 pounds) and super expensive (like six-figures expensive). Moog unveiled the first commercial synthesizer—the Moog synthesizer—at the Audio Engineering Society in New York in 1964, and the compact-sized device playable by a keyboard transformed everything. The Moog synthesizer made appearances on albums by The Monkees, The Rolling Stones, The Doors, and other iconic bands. Head to Moog Music for a factory tour, and see the craftspeople lovingly work their magic. Each synthesizer is made by hand using wood sourced from Tennessee and metal from Missouri. Add Moogseum to your list for an in-depth look at the birth of synthesizers, Moog's life and innovations, and other equipment that altered music in the '60s and '70s.

160 Broadway St., (828) 239-0123
moogmusic.com

56 Broadway St., (828) 258-1262
moogseum.org

HIT THE TRAIL
FOR URBAN ART

Though launched in 2016, the Appalachian Mural Trail is the result of 10 years of research conducted by founders Jerry and artist Doreyl Ammons Cain. The trail showcases the modest Appalachian towns and communities that display their culture, history, and tales through colorful outdoor (and indoor) art. Asheville is home to six murals included on the trail. The Haywood Street Fresco, located in Haywood Street Methodist Church, is a timely perspective of Jesus's "Beatitudes" sermon. Historic frescoes often depicted wealthy patrons or notable political figures. However, the 31 portraits included in this work were drawn from the Haywood Street community—those who have endured homelessness, poverty, addiction, and other hardships. A larger-than-life Dolly Parton Mural is a fitting tribute to the talented songstress and country music icon. It's located at the corner of Mildred Avenue and Haywood Road. It's hard to miss the 10-foot-tall rooster on the Chicken Alley Mural. It pays homage to the chicken processing plant for which the alley is named. The Lexington Avenue Gateway Mural canvases the six concrete piers supporting the I-240 bridges over Broadway Avenue. Located on South Market Street, the Triangle Park Mural captures the stories of the African American community. The three-paneled Shindig on the Green Mural ("Golden Threads") highlights the artists within Western North Carolina's traditional music culture.

(828) 293-2239
muraltrail.com

CHECK OUT EVEN MORE ART

Though this list indicates murals listed on the Appalachian Mural Trail, art is almost incidental in Asheville. Keep your eyes open for smaller murals and works of art on display throughout the city. Drive through the River Arts District for vibrant and creative public art. Seek out Tom Selleck and Sloth from the movie *The Goonies* at Burial Beer Co. Look up as you pass by the north entrance of the Aloft Hotel parking garage at 51 Biltmore for a peek at a daydreamer.

Haywood Street Fresco
297 Haywood St., (828) 575-2477
haywoodstreet.org

Dolly Parton Mural
783 Haywood Rd.

Chicken Alley Mural
4 Woodfin St.

Lexington Avenue Gateway Mural
Milepost 384 off the Blue Ridge Pkwy.

Triangle Park Mural
50 S Market St.

Shindig on the Green Mural — "Golden Threads"
Milepost 384 off the Blue Ridge Pkwy.

GET YOUR ART FIX
AT MUSEUMS AND GALLERIES

The talent in Western North Carolina is almost staggering. Asheville is a hub for creative thinkers and gifted makers, so you'd be wise to devote some time exploring them here. Established by artists in 1948, the Asheville Art Museum is the third oldest art museum in North Carolina. Originally situated on Charlotte Street in E.W. Grove's former land sales office, the museum moved and expanded over the years. Its new home (opened in 2019) is located at Pack Square. They offer an impressive schedule of exhibitions showcasing 20th- and 21st-century American art. The Appalachian Craft Center has supported local potters for over 40 years. Today, more than 150 craftspeople from all over the state and the Southern Appalachians are represented. Peruse glass art, books by local artists, locally made jewelry, homemade jams, jellies, and other homegrown gifts. Regular demonstrations allow visitors the chance to watch artisans create their masterpieces. The experimental school Black Mountain College was the place for pioneering artists, musicians, and writers in the mid-20th century. The 6,500-square-foot Black Mountain College Museum and Art Center shares the college's historic contributions through exhibitions, seminars, films, and performances.

Asheville Art Museum	Appalachian Craft Center	Black Mountain College
2 S Pack Square,	10 N Spruce St.,	Museum and Art Center
(828) 253-3227	(828) 253-8499	120 College St.,
ashevilleart.org	appalachiancraft	(828) 350-8484
	center.com	blackmountaincollege.org

Visited w/ Julie 08/05/21.

EXPLORE
HISTORIC GROVEWOOD VILLAGE

If you're into history, furniture, arts and design, clothing, or cars, this is a must-visit. Listed on the National Register of Historic Places, Grovewood Village once housed Biltmore Industries, Inc.'s woodworking and weaving operations. In its heyday in the late 1920s, the company produced 950 yards of fabric every day, employing around 100 workers. Today the village comprises Biltmore Industries Homespun Museum, working artist studios, galleries, the Estes-Winn Antique Car Museum, and Golden Fleece restaurant. The Biltmore Industries Homespun Museum illuminates the history of locally produced fabric through a film, exhibits, and a guided tour of the Dye House. Get to know the resident artists and their work during a free, self-guided tour of their studios. The artists represent a variety of art mediums. The Estes-Winn Antique Car Museum is a treasure trove for classic car buffs. You'll find a 1957 Cadillac Eldorado Brougham (only 400 were made!) and other vintage gems. Grovewood Gallery is open all year, though the museums close from January to March. Admission and parking for Grovewood Village are both free.

TIP
Grovewood Village is a short walk from the Omni Grove Park Inn. When you finish your time at the village, take a self-guided tour of the inn and learn more about its fascinating history and the impact of the Arts and Crafts Movement in the inn's décor.

SOAK IN
THE BUSKING SCENE

As you stroll around downtown Asheville, music often spills out of bars and restaurants. But if you spend any time in Pack Square, you'll get to soak in the varied talents of Asheville's buskers. Defined as the activity of playing music in the street or other public places for donations, busking is one of my favorite things about Asheville. Enjoy American folk and roots music from The Fly By Night Rounders, comprised of Abby the Spoon Lady, Chris Rodrigues, and Vaden Landers. Stop by and let poet Eddie Cabbage write you a poem. Jazz musician Andrew Fletcher serenades passersby with his trusty piano, Emily. Take a selfie with living statue Dade Murphy. Buskers are often out from late morning until around 9 p.m. Other popular spots to soak in the busking scene are in front of the Flat Iron sculpture on Wall Street at Battery Park Avenue, in front of Woolworth Walk on Haywood Street, and by the Grove Arcade.

TIP
Make sure to have cash on hand so you can tip the performers. They work hard at what they do—show you appreciate them sharing their talent!

●　●　●　●　●　●　●　●　●　●　●　●　●　●　●　●　●　●　●

PUSH
YOUR BOUNDARIES
AT THE ASHEVILLE FRINGE
ARTS FESTIVAL

The movement began in 1947 in Edinburgh, Scotland. The city's mainstream arts festival excluded eight performing companies, so they decided to perform anyway on the outskirts of the city. The Edinburgh Fringe Festival eventually overshadowed the original festival, becoming one of the world's largest arts festivals. Fringe festivals popped up all over the place—Asia, Europe, Canada, and the US. Inspired by Fringe festivals they had attended in Toronto and San Francisco, founders Susan and Giles Collard decided it was time Asheville hosted their own. The Asheville Fringe Arts Festival showcases edgy and original performances from local and imported artists. Modern dance, sketch theater, singing, dancing, puppetry, painting, and others—there's a wealth of opportunity to be engaged and inspired.

20 Commerce St., (828) 254-2621
ashevillefringe.org

MARCH TO THE BEAT
OF YOUR OWN DRUM
IN PRITCHARD PARK

The almost 20-year-old Public Drum Circle began with just about 10 drummers, and has evolved into one of Asheville's best-loved community traditions. Every Friday at around 6 p.m. (April through October), folks converge in Pritchard Park for a public jam session. The session begins with a core group of musicians, but anyone can participate. Sway to the rhythm of djembes, congas, shekeres, dunduns, and other instruments—or bring your own and join in. It's a free event, and usually lasts until 10 p.m.

Patton Ave. at College St.
facebook.com/groups/2417488508

SEE ASHEVILLE
IN THE MOVIES

With its small-town charm, scenic landscapes, and a local "castle," it's no surprise Asheville has been a lure for film directors since 1921. The town played prominently in the 1921 silent movie *Conquest of Canaan*. The film serves as a scrapbook of sorts for the Asheville of yesteryear. Pack Square, the Patton-Parker House, and the old Swannanoa-Berkeley Hotel (site of today's Aloft) make an appearance. Biltmore House premiered on the big screen in 1956 in the movie *The Swan*, starring Grace Kelly and Alec Guinness. Biltmore Estate went on to appear in *Being There* (1979), *Mr. Destiny* (1990), *Richie Rich* (1994), *Patch Adams* (1998), *Hannibal* (2001), and others. *Last of the Mohicans* was also filmed at Biltmore Estate, as well as at locations outside of Asheville—Dupont State Forest and Chimney Rock Park. Portions of Forrest Gump's iconic running scene in the Academy Award-winning movie were shot on the road at Grandfather Mountain. (The area is now called "The Forrest Gump Curve.") Just outside Asheville, the abandoned Henry River mill village became the backdrop for District 12 in the 2011 blockbuster hit *The Hunger Games*. Filming for the 2016 comedy *Masterminds* took place in downtown Asheville. The former BB&T building served as the movie's "Park Street Citizens Bank." Also, portions of the 2015 movie *The Longest Ride*, based on the Nicholas Sparks novel, were filmed at The Omni Grove Park Inn.

SUPPORT LOCAL ARTISTS
AT THE FOLK ART CENTER

Hop off the Blue Ridge Parkway and milepost 382 and be awed by an incredible collection of contemporary and traditional craft art. The center is headquarters for the Southern Highland Craft Guild, comprised of more than 900 juried artists from across the Southeast. Formed in 1930, the Guild was created to serve as a network for Appalachian craftspeople and offer an outlet to market their work. It's also home to the Allanstand Craft Shop, the Guild's oldest craft store, and one of the first of its kind in the United States. Head upstairs for a look at 250 crafts from the Guild's permanent collection—some dating from the mid-1800s. Other rotating galleries showcase various artists, and you'll find an extensive selection of unique works in the Southern Highland Craft Guild store—from paintings, pottery, and wood crafts to jewelry, quilts, and glass art.

Milepost 382, Blue Ridge Pkwy., (828) 298-7909
southernhighlandguild.org

EXTRA CREDIT
The Folk Art Center's parking area also accesses the Mountains-to-Sea Trail. When you finish your visit, spend time outside appreciating Mother Nature's artwork!

Visited

GO WITH THE FLOW
IN THE RIVER ARTS DISTRICT

This one-mile stretch of about 22 former industrial buildings along the French Broad River is home to galleries and studios where hundreds of artists showcase their work representing a huge variety of styles and mediums. The buildings operated for decades as cotton mills, tanneries, and other businesses. Many are painted with vibrant graffiti created by local and national artists. You'll discover a bevy of talented sculptors, potters, blacksmiths, weavers, furniture makers, and glassblowers here. Virtually everything here is crafted on-site, too. Learn from the masters with artist talks and classes. The district is extremely walkable—it's one of Asheville's most pedestrian-friendly neighborhoods. Close out your arts tour with a stop in one of the area's local breweries or restaurants.

(828) 552-4723
riverartsdistrict.com

CATCH A SHOW
AT GREY EAGLE MUSIC HALL

Originally located in Black Mountain, The Grey Eagle was housed in the garage and paint room of a former Chevrolet dealership. The venue moved to Asheville in 1999 and has been rocking out ever since as Asheville's longest-running live music venue for all ages. Even a pandemic can't stop the music. During the COVID-19 lockdown, Grey Eagle continued to support local musicians by livestreaming shows from the stage. Over the years, they've hosted Avett Brothers, Dap Kings, Ralph Stanley, and others, as well as a huge list of local bands and artists—more than 10,000 of them. Sometimes the artist isn't always on stage. Actors Russell Crowe and Adam Goldberg were spotted enjoying an Alex Cameron performance last year.

Before the show, grab a bite at Tacqueria, located inside. They serve authentic Latin American fare with gluten-free and vegan options. You don't have to wait for a show to enjoy Tacqueria. It's open Tuesday through Sunday from noon to 8 p.m. Graze on traditional-style tacos like chorizo, shrimp, mahi-mahi, carne asada, and others. Grab a taco off their vegan menu—cauliflower, black bean and sweet potato, or lentil chorizo. Burritos and quesadillas are also offered. Wash it down with a local craft beer or an insanely good fresh-made margarita.

185 Clingman Ave., (828) 232-5800
thegreyeagle.com

LAY DOWN A TRACK
AT AMERICAN VINYL CO.

Listening to your music via a digital music service is convenient, but it just can't hold a candle to the crackle and hiss of a vintage vinyl spinning on a turntable. That thought was the impetus behind American Vinyl Co. Musicians and sound engineers Christy Barrett and Ryan Schilling are the architects who create custom vinyl records for anyone and everyone. A song, comedy skit, poem—whatever you want to share, they can make a field recording of it. You can certainly dream bigger, though. Among some of the most unique recordings they've done include a lady having a baby and a completely silent record used for meditation or ASMR. They offer two different processes. One is the lathe cut record where they cut the audio to a PVC disc over and over. The quantities are smaller, allowing for shorter production time (two to four weeks). Plating involves taking the master disc and creating a negative from it. They use the final negative to put into a record press and press the grooves into PVC. This process is about an eight-week turnaround. Short on time? Record your song live on vinyl in their American Sound Truck, their 1950s recording studio built into a van. You leave that day with your very own record!

22 London Rd., (828) 367-7354
americanvinylco.com

MEET A MOTLEY FOOL
WITH MONTFORD PARK PLAYERS

A production of William Shakespeare's *As You Like It* performed in a city park in 1973 launched a legacy of theatric proportions. Founded by Hazel Robinson, Montford Park Players is one of just 15 theaters in the world to have staged every one of Shakespeare's plays. The group expanded their repertoire over the years, performing classically inspired plays, but their Shakespeare roots remain strong. Montford Park Players boasts the longest-running Shakespeare festival in the state. Sit under the stars on a summer night and revel in a Shakespeare performance at the outdoor amphitheater named for the group's visionary founder. Pack a picnic, or purchase a snack at concessions. Bring a chair and arrive early for the best seat up front. Fall and winter plays take place at the historic Masonic Temple.

Summer: 92 Gay St.
Winter: 80 Broadway St.
(828) 254-2663
montfordparkplayers.org

TIP

Montford Park Players is a
federally recognized, 501(c)3 not-for-
profit organization. That means you get
to enjoy each performance for free. They
pass around the hat at intermission, so
make sure and bring your cash (and be
generous!). You can also support
them monthly or annually.

HOP ON
THE GRAY LINE TROLLEY

Whether you want to get an educational and entertaining insight to Asheville or are looking for a fun themed experience, a narrated tour with Gray Line Trolley is the way to go. Locally owned and operated, they've been sharing Asheville with visitors and locals since 2007 (the Gray Line company dates back to 1910). It's a great family-friendly diversion, too, as kids aged four and under ride free. The 90 Minute Overview Tour is the ideal way to kick off any visit to Asheville, and it's endorsed by the Preservation Society of Asheville and Buncombe County, so you know it's legit! The tour route hits more than 100 points of interest—historic spots, notable homes, popular hangouts, and others. You can customize your own experience with the Hop On/Hop Off Tour, which gives you unlimited hop-on/hop-off privileges at 10 stops. Learn all about the spirits, murders, and intriguing history of Asheville during a Haunted History & Murder Mystery Ghost Tour. The Christmas Tour is the perfect way to usher in the holidays, complete with a tour of holiday decorations, storytelling and caroling. Don't worry if you're rusty in the Christmas songs department—they provide song sheets!

36 Montford Ave., (828) 251-TOUR (8687)
graylineasheville.com

RING IN THE HOLIDAYS
AT THE OMNI GROVE PARK INN NATIONAL GINGERBREAD HOUSE COMPETITION

It began in 1992 as a small display of gingerbread houses created by Asheville locals. More than two decades later, this Asheville tradition has become the largest gingerbread competition in the world. Competitors across the country pour their heart, soul, and lots of sugar into their creations. The gingerbread entries don't have to be a house. Past entries have included a pirate ship, a typewriter, a grandfather clock, and a table of reindeer playing poker. However, they must be completely edible—and made up of at least 75 percent gingerbread. Renowned celebrity chef Carla Hall is among the competition's panel of judges. Due to COVID-19, the 2020 competition was held virtually, offering socially distant experiences for hotel guests and visitors.

290 Macon Ave., (800) 413-5778
omnihotels.com/hotels/Asheville-grove-park

08/21/21 w/ Julie.

WALK ALONG
WALL STREET

Historic Wall Street might be one of my favorite areas to spend an afternoon. Nestled between Battery Park and Patton Avenue, this pedestrian-friendly street serves up low-key European vibes. The area was initially hailed as "the little street with big ideas" in its early days around the mid-'70s and through the '80s. Today, there's a good selection of shops, restaurants, and other diversions here. The Asheville Emporium has a little bit of everything, from locally made souvenirs to globally procured gifts. Clothing, stationery, artwork—you name it. Another favorite is Dolce Vita, which offers a good selection of bags and purses, jewelry, clothing, candles, and other gifts. Find custom-made sandals, wallets, and other items at Paul Taylor Sandals. Enjoy a craft beer, coffee, or a snack over a friendly game of Battleship or Monopoly at Well Played Board Game Café. Need to relax? Indulge in a bliss-inducing treatment at Blomkraft Studio. When you're ready to refuel, there's a good variety: Early Girl Eatery (Southern fare and breakfast all day), Laughing Seed Café (vegetarian sandwiches, salads, and family-style meals), Market Place (farm-to-fork goodness), Cucina 24 (upscale Italian and great cocktails), and Trade and Lore Coffee (specialty coffees, pastries, and craft beer).

EXTRA CREDIT
During your Wall Street walk, see if you can spy one of the bronze sculptures that comprise the "Cat Walk," one of the stations along the Urban Trail.

HERE'S WHERE TO STOP ON WALL STREET

Asheville Emporium
35 Wall St., (828) 785-5722
asheville-emporium.com

Dolce Vita
34 Wall St., Ste. 201, (828) 253-1584
dolcevitaavl.com

Paul Taylor Sandals
12 Wall St., (828) 251-0057
paultaylorsandals.com

Well Played Board Game Café
58 Wall St., (828) 232-7375
wellplayedasheville.com

Blomkraft Studio
12 ½ Wall St., Ste. F, (828) 595-3945
blomkraftstudio.com

Early Girl Eatery
8 Wall St., (828) 259-9292
earlygirleatery.com

Laughing Seed Café
40 Wall St., (828) 252-3445
laughingseed.com

Market Place
20 Wall St., (828) 252-4162
marketplace-restaurant.com

Cucina 24
24 Wall St., (828) 254-6170
cucina24restaurant.com

Trade and Lore Coffee
37 Wall St., (828) 552-5353
tradeandlore.com

Years ago w/ Honey.   08/21/21 w/ Julie,

ROVE AROUND
HISTORIC GROVE ARCADE

Spanning a city block, this Asheville landmark features a variety of specialty shops and restaurants that will likely lure you in for hours. Constructed between 1926 and 1929, it was originally designed to be the base of a skyscraper that never materialized. The ornate architecture is stunning, accentuated by a glass ceiling that fills the space with natural light. When Grove Arcade opened in 1929, it included a haberdashery, fruit stands, bookstalls, candy and cigar stores, specialty groceries, and other shops. The building closed in 1945, but was lovingly restored and reopened in 2002. Today you'll find an almost limitless selection of unique shops and several dining options. Browse pottery, blown glass, hand-painted silks, and other items crafted by more than 80 local artisans in Mountain Made. Channel your inner musician at The Woodrow Instrument Co. The Woodrow is a variation of the mountain dulcimer and easy to learn. Ask for a quick lesson when you visit, or just appreciate the handcrafted instruments they sell. Take a shopping break and reward your feet with a soak at Wake Foot Sanctuary. Sink into a thick, soft chair and inhale the soothing fragrance from your salt-based foot bath. Feeling peckish? Dine at Baba Nahm, Asheville Proper, Burgerworx, Carmel's Kitchen & Bar, Modesto, or Battery Park Book Exchange & Champagne Bar.

1 Page Ave., (828) 252-7799
grovearcade.com

TIP

Don't miss spending time at the Makers Market, located on the building's south side. This outdoor bazaar features a rotating selection of stalls filled with the work of some of the most talented artisans in the area. Shop for paintings, handmade soaps, local honey and produce, clothing, honey, and more. You'll find something different every time you visit, so go often!

SEE CLEARLY
AT LEXINGTON GLASSWORKS

Glassblowing techniques were invented around the first century B.C. by Syrian craftsmen along the Syro-Palestinian coast. Throughout the years, glassblowers were often held hostage so their knowledge of the art would be kept secret. Phoenician glassworkers were even forbidden to travel during the first century A.D. Thankfully, that has changed. Not only can glassblowers share their knowledge, but visitors to Lexington Glassworks can sneak a peek while they work. Observing the talent and effort that goes into making one of their pieces provides a greater appreciation for the art and the creative process. Their designs display exquisite patterns and vibrant colors in a variety of different styles—bottles, vases, bowls, glasses, ornaments, and more. Watch them work Monday and Wednesday through Saturday from 10 a.m. to 6 p.m. and on Sunday from 11 a.m. to 6 p.m. Lexington Glassworks also plays host to local art and bluegrass music, and serves craft beer every first Friday, from April through December.

81 S Lexington Ave., (828) 348-8427
lexingtonglassworks.com

ZOOM AROUND THE CITY
IN A PURPLE BUS

One of the most endearing qualities of Asheville is that most folks don't take themselves too seriously. LaZoom Tours has been cracking people up for 14 years. Board one of the open-air purple buses, and their hilarious tour guides will share all of Asheville's interesting and quirky bits. Tours also feature costumed characters and live onboard music. Every wacky comedy skit is different and written completely in-house. Comedy bus tours geared toward more mature humor include the City Tour, Band and Beer Tour, and the Haunted Tour. A Kids' Comedy Tour is age appropriate and a ton of fun. They also offer a walking ghost tour.

76 Biltmore Ave., (828) 225-6932
lazoomtours.com

GRAB A SEAT
AT SILVER RIVER CHAIRS

Dating as far back as 1300 B.C., the craft of caning chairs is a form of basketry applied to the back and seat of chairs. Silver River Chairs is the only chair caning school and museum in the country. Owners Brandy Clements and Dave Klinger aim to enlighten visitors on this traditional art, as well as revive the art of chair caning. There's no charge for the working museum. You can watch them work and ask questions along the way. For a more in-depth experience, sign up for one of their chair weaving and caning classes, or learn how to make a whisk broom.

#5 River Arts Place, Ste. 201, (828) 707-4553
silverriverchairs.com

GET INTO THE SWING OF THINGS
AT EMPYREAN ARTS

When co-owners Waverly Jones and Heather Poole discovered aerial silks classes, they both fell in love instantly. Jones grew up doing gymnastics, and Poole's background included acrobatics, yoga, and Pilates. The two joined forces in 2015 to create Empyrean Arts, offering specialized movement arts and alternative fitness classes. You don't need to be a pro. They offer classes for all levels—from trapeze, aerial arts, and pole fitness to strength training, flexibility, and therapeutic movement. The only skill required is the desire to be stronger, more flexible, and more confident. You can join a small group session or opt for a private one-on-one class. They also host private parties (girls' weekend getaway, anyone?).

32 Banks Ave., (828) 782-3321
empyreanarts.org

STAY UP LATE
FOR NIGHTLIFE

There's no shortage of places to enjoy Asheville's nightlife. If you can't decide between chilling out and getting your groove on, O. Henry's is the place to go. Established in 1976, this landmark is the first and oldest gay bar in North Carolina. O. Henry's has transcended its early days as a local sandwich shop. It quickly became known as being gay-friendly, and continues to be a favorite club for locals and visitors alike. Hang out at the front of the club for a low-key, neighborhood bar atmosphere, or head back to The Underground, the lively industrial dance bar. If craft cocktails are your thing, Rankin Vault Cocktail Lounge can deliver. One glance at their custom walnut bar transports you to a bygone era. As the name implies, a Mosler Safe Company bank vault provides a room for parties up to 12 people. Sample signature cocktails like Dr. Hannah's Purple Pill (Beefeater gin, Crème de Violette, St. Germain Elderflower Liqueur, lemon, and lavender syrup). The cocktails are on point, but don't ignore their food menu. They've snagged first-place People's Choice at the WNC Battle of the Burger five years in a row. Their selection of tacos, burgers, salads, and appetizers will fuel you as you socialize.

O. Henry's	Rankin Vault Cocktail Lounge
237 Haywood St., (828) 254-1891	7 Rankin Ave., (828) 254-4993
ohenrysofasheville.com	rankinvault.com

NERD OUT
AT THE ASHEVILLE MUSEUM OF SCIENCE

Though small, this science learning center is a big draw for families. Admission is just $8 for adults and $7 for kids, seniors, and students, making it a fun and budget-friendly activity for everyone. Engineer and bank president Burnham Standish Colburn, who retired to Asheville in the 1920s, was the inspiration behind the museum. An avid mineralogist, Colburn and his brother helped form the Southern Appalachian Mineral Society in 1931. Upon Colburn's death, his family shared his collections with the public through the Burnham S. Colburn Memorial Museum. Opened in 2016, the Asheville Museum of Science continues his legacy. Minerals and cut gemstones from around the world are on display here, as well as some 350 minerals discovered in North Carolina—quartz, mica, corundum, sapphire, emerald, hiddenite, and topaz are just a few to admire. You'll also find fully interactive exhibits and educational programs that provide insight into geology, weather, astronomy, climate, and paleontology. The Asheville Museum of Science is housed in the Wells Fargo Building on the corner of Battery Park and Patton Avenue.

43 Patton Ave., (828) 254-7162
ashevillescience.org

Stand-Up Paddleboarding
Photo courtesy of exploreasheville.com

SPORTS AND RECREATION

CHEER ON RUNNERS
AT THE ASHEVILLE MARATHON

Whether you're an avid race junkie or just want to support your runner friends, this is the race for you. Unlike many courses that often run along asphalt highways or city roads, this course runs through America's largest backyard. Running entirely on Biltmore Estate property, the course even weaves through areas not normally open to Biltmore Estate visitors. Exceptional views of the estate, gorgeous gardens, the pastoral banks of the French Broad River—there's plenty of beauty to distract you from the challenge of completing the 26.2-mile race. There's also a 13.1 half marathon that follows a similar route.

asthevillemarathon.com

TAKE YOURSELF OUT TO THE BALLGAME
AT MCCORMICK FIELD

Named after prominent local doctor Lewis McCormick, McCormick Field opened in 1924. The Asheville Tourists, the city's Minor League Baseball team, played until the city lost its franchise in 1933 during the height of the Great Depression. Over the next several years, the field played host to exhibition games by the likes of the New York Yankees (with Babe Ruth and Lou Gehrig) and the Brooklyn Dodgers (with Jackie Robinson). The Asheville Tourists came back in 1959, but Asheville baseball suffered in the 1970s due to low attendance and rowdy fans. Ron McKee brought new life to the game in 1980 when he became general manager, creating a more family-friendly environment and offering fun giveaways and clever promotions. More than 180,000 Tourists fans come out each year.

30 Buchanan Pl., (828) 258-0428
milb.com/Asheville

BE A PINBALL WIZARD
AT THE ASHEVILLE PINBALL MUSEUM

Kids and adults who feel like kids will want to spend time at perhaps one of Asheville's most unique places. It's situated in the historic Battery Park Hotel Building, which went up in 1924 and is listed on the National Register of Historic Places. Part arcade, part museum, the Pinball Museum houses more than 30 vintage pinball machines and 20-plus video games. Some date back to the 1930s. There's no charge to look, and one price gets you in to play—no quarters needed! Adults pay $15, and children 10 and under play for $12. They also offer snacks, drinks, and beer.

1 Battle Square, Ste. 1B, (828) 776-5671
pinball.ashevillepinball.com

DON'T STOP
YOUR BELLYAKING

The best ideas happen when we least expect it. That was certainly the case with Adam Masters, founder of the Bellyak. When a hurricane blew through his home in South Carolina several years ago, the creek by his home swelled to the brink. The rhododendrons along the creek made it impossible to ride the rapids in a kayak, so Masters duct-taped the top and paddled on his belly. Through the years, he perfected his idea, and Bellyak was born in 2013. Bellyak is the perfect marriage of swimming and kayaking. You paddle on your stomach, using webbed "paddle gloves" to help move you along. Adventurers of all skill levels can participate. Also, in 2014, the company introduced adaptive paddling. You can Bellyak on the river, in the ocean, or on a lake. They only weigh about 30 pounds, making them easy to carry anywhere.

1465 Sand Hill Rd., Candler, (828) 231-7469
bellyak.com

GET SALTY
AT THE ASHEVILLE SALT CAVE

For centuries, salt therapy has been used for healing and wellness. Hippocrates recommended salt inhalation as an effective treatment for respiratory problems. Polish physician Felix Boczkowski discovered that salt mine workers had fewer respiratory issues than others, which he traced back to the inhalation of the salt dust. At the Asheville Salt Cave, you can step into a cozy grotto made of 20 tons of pure pink salt. The cave salt is procured from all over the world—the Dead Sea, Himalayan Mountains, Polish salt mines and the Celtic Sea. They've naturally recreated the micro climate of a salt mine, maintaining the exact temperature and humidity of a cave. You're soothed by the dim glow from rock lamps. Lay on the salt floor, or relax in a zero-gravity chair. For complete relaxation, pair your salt cave session with a massage or specialty treatment like hot salt stone therapy. They also offer balance restorative energy healing sessions. You can do a public session or book a private one. Chill with your kids on Sundays with a Kids Quiet Place Session.

16 N Liberty St., (828) 236-5999
ashevillesaltcave.com

TIP

They also offer hammam—a Middle Eastern variant of a steam bath. It's designed to exfoliate and detoxify your skin, as well as refresh your mind. Decorative tile adorns the walls of the steam room. Pamper yourself with a traditional hammam service provided by a staff member, or do your own.

TALK TO THE ANIMALS
AT ANIMAL HAVEN OF ASHEVILLE

For more than 20 years, this idyllic farm sanctuary has been a saving grace for animals that have been neglected, abused, and abandoned. The 10-acre property includes a tranquil stream, a pond, and a smattering of small red barns that serve as homes for the animals. While most of their residents are rescued farm animals, they also care for cats and dogs that need to be adopted. In addition to caring for the animals, Animal Haven hosts educational programs for all ages that focus on responsible pet ownership, as well as enlighten people on the true condition and treatment of farm animals. Spend the day visiting goats, potbellied pigs, chickens, and other sweet creatures. Don't miss their well-stocked, 1,500-square-foot thrift shop filled with jewelry, books, clothing, furniture, collectibles, pet supplies, and other items. The sanctuary is completely volunteer-run, and they receive no federal or state funding. Profits from the thrift store help offset their expenses.

65 Lower Grassy Branch Rd., (828) 299-1635
animalhavenofasheville.org

FLOAT DOWN
THE FRENCH BROAD

Winding through the center of Asheville and running north, the French Broad River is believed to be the third oldest river in the world. Most of the river provides a gentle flow of water, with occasional sections offering classes I and II rapids. There are many ways to enjoy this 200-mile-long waterway—kayak, canoe, tube, SUP, and raft—and local river outfitters offer guided trips. Asheville Outdoor Center offers a seven-mile trip that takes you by Biltmore Estate, offering a different view of the grounds from the water. Choose a six-mile Biltmore tour, six-mile River Arts District tour, or opt for a 12-mile combo via kayak or canoe with French Broad Outfitters. The River Arts District tour offers a SUP option. Take a tubing tour, and let the river's current do all the work. Spring for a cooler float for $5 and enjoy a cold beverage along the way. Nantahala Outdoor Center offers both half- and full-day (and family-friendly) white water rafting excursions. Some tours include lunch on the riverbank. You can always hit the river on your own using your personal kayak or canoe, or renting one from one of the local outfitters. Hominy Creek River Park and Bent Creek River Park are a couple of good launching points.

Asheville Outdoor Center	French Broad Outfitters	Nantahala Outdoor Center
521 Amboy Rd.,	704 Riverside Dr.,	9825 US-25, Marshall,
(828) 232-1970	(828) 505-7371	(828) 348-8744
ashevilleoutdoorcenter.com	frenchbroadoutfitters.com	noc.com

GET SPOOKED ON A GHOST TOUR
WITH HAUNTED ASHEVILLE

When 18-year-old Joshua Warren authored and published the first book of Asheville ghost stories in 1996, the public clearly wanted more. The book, *Haunted Asheville*, became the number-one regional bestseller within days of its release. (It's also the most stolen book in the history of the Buncombe County Library System.) Warren received an overwhelming number of requests from readers who wanted to visit the places he described in the book. With that, Asheville's first and oldest ghost tour company was established. Tour guides are engaging and well-versed in all things paranormal, providing you a deeper look into Asheville's haunted history. Three tours are on offer: The Classic Walking Tour (learn about the body entombed in the wall of St. Lawrence and other spine tinglers); The Supernatural Tour (reveals local legends about witches, vampires, and demons); and The Biltmore Village Mystery Tour (hear about the curse of George Vanderbilt's lawyer, Samuel Reed). Haunted Asheville has earned the Tripadvisor Travelers' Choice award for the past five years and was featured in *USA Today's 10Best* as one of the top ghost tours in America in 2020.

80 Broadway St., (828) 318-8579
hauntedasheville.com

TEE OFF
WITH A ROUND OF GOLF

The mountain landscape and altitude changes in Asheville create an incredible backdrop for any game, any season. Spring gives way to blooming flowers and lush forests. Vibrant shades of gold, maroon, and red greet fall golfers. The 18-hole Omni Grove Park Inn Golf Course opened in 1899 and was redesigned by Donald Ross in 1926. For more than 20 years, it was a regular PGA Tour stop. Golf greats Ben Hogan, Jack Nicklaus, and Bobby Jones have enjoyed games here, and President Obama teed it up during his Asheville vacation in 2018. The course received a complete renovation in 2011, yet still maintains its historic feel. With gorgeous views of the grand resort and sweeping vistas of the Blue Ridge Mountains beyond, golfers are surrounded in splendor. The Asheville Municipal Golf Course is another Donald Ross creation. Built in 1927, it's one of the state's oldest golf courses and listed on the National Register of Historic Places. The course follows the Swannanoa River and offers scenic Blue Ridge Mountains views.

Omni Grove Park Inn Golf Course
290 Macon Ave., (828) 252-2711
omnihotels.com/hotels/asheville-grove-park

Asheville Municipal Golf Course
226 Fairway Dr., (828) 298-1867
ashevillegc.com

GO
TO THE DOGS

As you walk along the streets of Asheville, you'll likely notice a number of water-filled dog bowls outside of shops and restaurants. Some venues even offer dog treats for your four-legged companions. Asheville is extremely pet-friendly. And let's be honest, isn't everything we do a little more fun with our pets? Make your first stop Dog City, U.S.A., the city's official welcome center for dogs. Located within the Dog Door Store, welcome center staff will give you a goody cup with a brochure that lists information on dog-friendly everything in Asheville. They also offer a dog tour of downtown dog-friendly shops and breweries, with an area map, a poop bag, and a treat sample, as well as a list of hiking trails open to four-legged, leashed hikers. Dog parks like Azalea Dog Park and French Broad River Dog Park are great spots to let Fido be his active and playful self. Many breweries like French Broad River Brewery, Archetype Brewing, Eurisko Beer Company, and others allow dogs to hang out with you while you enjoy your beer. Seeing the sights on the trolley? Well-behaved pets are allowed on the historic Gray Line Asheville Trolley Tours. Pamper your good boy with treats and cool pet gear at Patton Avenue Pet Company West. If you're overnighting it, The Omni Grove Park Inn, Aloft Asheville Downtown, and The Black Walnut Bed & Breakfast Inn are a few of several pet-friendly accommodations in the area.

HERE'S WHERE YOU CAN BRING FIDO ALONG

Dog City, U.S.A.
1 Battle Sq., Ste. A, (828) 398-1868
dogdoorcanineservices.com

Azalea Dog Park
395 Azalea Rd.

French Broad River Dog Park
180 Amboy Rd.

French Broad River Brewery
101 Fairview Rd., #D, (828) 277-0222
frenchbroadbrewery.com

Archetype Brewing
174 Broadway St., (828) 505-8305
archetypebrewing.com

Eurisko Beer Company
255 Short Coxe Ave., (828) 774-5055
euriskobeer.com

Historic Gray Line Asheville Trolley Tours
36 Montford Ave., (828) 251-TOUR (8687)
graylineasheville.com

Patton Avenue Pet Company West
1388 Patton Ave., (828) 505-8299
pattonavenuepet.com

The Omni Grove Park Inn
290 Macon Rd., (828) 252-2711
omnihotels.com/hotels/asheville-grove-park

Aloft Asheville Downtown
51 Biltmore Ave., (828) 232-2838
marriott.com/hotels/travel/avlal-aloft-
asheville-downtown

The Black Walnut Bed & Breakfast Inn
288 Montford Ave., (828) 254-3878
blackwalnut.com

GO GHOST HUNTING
ALONG HELEN'S BRIDGE

Located on Beaucatcher Road overlooking downtown Asheville, Helen's Bridge is believed to have been haunted for nearly 100 years. It was constructed in 1909 to connect Zealandia Mansion (built in 1908) to the roadways leading to the rest of Asheville. Thomas Wolfe mentions the bridge in his novel *Look Homeward, Angel*. Helen is believed to have lived at or near the mansion with her only daughter. Stories vary on what drove her to hang herself from one of the bridge's steel posts. Some say she was inconsolable from losing her daughter in a house fire. Others believe she was a pregnant single woman who was rejected by her married lover. Some have witnessed a shadowy figure moving back and forth along the bridge. Some drivers who pass under the bridge have reported drained batteries, stalled engines, and other mechanical problems. Over the years, the bridge has been a popular spot for paranormal investigators and ghost hunters.

201 Beaucatcher Rd.

TIP
The Zealandia Mansion earned a spot on the National Register of Historic Places in 1977.

AMP UP YOUR CAMPING
WITH ASHEVILLE GLAMPING

Gone are the days where overnighting it in the great outdoors is associated with "roughing it." Glamping is the perfect answer to the quandary: "I'd like to go camping, but I do love my hotels." If you want to enjoy spending time outdoors, but need more comfort than the forest floor allows, glamping is a great alternative. All units have AC, and some include a heat source. Half of the sites share a bath house, while the other half includes private bathrooms (no running water). Guests can choose from whimsical accommodations like domes, yurts, revamped vintage trailers, and treehouses. The largest dome (1,300 square feet) sleeps up to eight people and features a fun sleeping loft with a nine-foot slide that brings you back down to the first floor. You can use the stairs, but why miss all the fun? Asheville Glamping has been featured on the Travel Channel, HGTV, *Good Morning America*, and others. They've also earned mentions in *Vogue*, *Outside*, *Country Living*, and *Southern Living* magazines.

(828) 450-9745
ashevilleglamping.com

TIP
If you're interested in a weekend stay in the Mega Dome or treehouse, book early. They are wildly popular sites and tend to book up to a year in advance.

STAY IN A GEM
AND SLEEP LIKE A KING

For more than 80 years, savvy travelers have relied on the AAA Diamond rating to vet their choice of accommodations. Extensive amenities, upscale rooms, and stellar hospitality are all hallmarks of hotels and bed-and-breakfasts earning the AAA Four Diamond rating, and Asheville boasts nine of them. Both The Inn on Biltmore Estate and The Omni Grove Park Inn are the longest-running properties to earn the Four Diamond distinction, beginning in 2001. Albemarle Inn snagged the title in 2003 (and every year since). In 2009, Asheville added Grand Bohemian Hotel Asheville, Autograph Collection and 1900 Inn on Montford to the prestigious list, followed by Hilton Asheville Biltmore Park in 2010. Biltmore Village Inn and 1889 WhiteGate Inn & Cottage received their Four Diamond status in 2011, followed by Abbington Green Bed & Breakfast Inn and Spa (2014).

BOOK A STAY AT THESE DIAMOND PROPERTIES

The Omni Grove Park Inn
290 Macon Ave., (800) 413-5778
omnihotels.com/hotels/Asheville-grove-park

The Inn on Biltmore Estate
One Lodge St., (800) 411-3812
biltmore.com/stay/the-inn/

Albemarle Inn
86 Edgemont Rd., (828) 255-0027
albemarleinn.com

Grand Bohemian Hotel Asheville
11 Boston Way, (828) 505-2949
kesslercollection.com/bohemian-asheville

1900 Inn on Montford
296 Montford Ave., #1660, (800) 254-9569
innonmontford.com

Hilton Asheville Biltmore Park
43 Town Square Blvd., (828) 209-2700
biltmorefarmshotels.com/Hilton-
asheville-biltmore-park

Biltmore Village Inn
119 Dodge St., (828) 274-8707
biltmorevillageinn.com

1889 WhiteGate Inn & Cottage
173 E Chestnut St., (828) 253-2553
whitegate.net

Abbington Green Bed & Breakfast Inn and Spa
46 Cumberland Cir., (828) 251-2454
abbingtongreen.com

Visited w/ Julie 08/05/21. Toured gardens, lunched @ the Bistro and did a 2 mi. hike. Very Nice.

GET LOST IN NATURE
AT THE N.C. ARBORETUM

Spanning some 434 acres abundant with vibrant flower gardens, lush grounds, and forest trails, the N.C. Arboretum offers a lovely escape for the day. Learn about Southern Appalachian plants historically used for natural dyes, basket making, broom making, and medicines in the Heritage Garden. The impressive Bonsai Exhibition Garden hosts up to 50 bonsai specimens at a time, and is an ideal spot for meditative contemplation. There are more than 10 miles of hiking and biking trails to explore. They connect to other outdoor attractions, such as the Pisgah National Forest and Lake Powhatan. Indoors, you can peruse an exhibition at the Baker Exhibit Center and take in unique artwork by regional artists and craftsmen in the Education Center. Rotating exhibits, art collections, and frequent events like lectures, plant shows, and engaging kids' programs mean you can visit often and see something new each time. You can easily spend a full day here. Purchase lunch on-site at Bent Creek Bistro, offering salads, sandwiches, and soups (all food is packed picnic-ready). Or, bring your own picnic fare and grab a spot anywhere on the 434-acre campus.

100 Frederick Law Olmsted Way, (828) 665-2492
ncarboretum.org

TIP
Admission is free, but parking is $16 (per car).
Every first Tuesday of the month, parking is $8.

TIP

Plan a visit during the holidays for the Winter Lights event. Be awed by 500,000 festive lights, illuminated displays throughout the gardens, and holiday music. Warm up with s'mores, hot chocolate, or a warm adult beverage. (Tickets are available at ncarboretum.org.)

STOP AND SMELL
THE FLOWERS
AT THE BOTANICAL GARDENS

Tucked within the city on the University of North Carolina at Asheville, the Botanical Gardens at Asheville offers a quiet garden retreat filled with more than 600 species native to the Southern Appalachians. The 10-acre gardens are rich with wildflowers, shrubs, and vines, as well as a robust collection of magnolia, native pine, and birch trees. They also have more than 70 species of plants considered rare or endangered, including French Broad Heartleaf, Oconee Bells, and Pale Yellow Trillium. An easy walking trail winds through meadows and over streams. A spring visit will yield color from spring bloomers like wild geranium, crested dwarf iris, and foamflower. Stroll the garden in midsummer or early fall for blooming Joe Pye weed, blazing star, goldenrod, and green-headed coneflower. If you have kids in tow, stop by the Visitor Center for an Investigative Passport filled with garden activities. Kids can get their passports stamped upon completion at the Visitor Center before they leave.

151 W.T. Weaver Blvd., (828) 252-5190
ashevillebotanicalgardens.org

TIP
Look for the "Moon Tree" at the west end of the garden. The tree was grown from the seed of a tree taken on the 1971 Apollo 14 lunar mission.

FIND YOUR CENTER
IN THE MOUNTAINS

Asheville has long been known as a community that nurtures and emphasizes the importance of health and wellness. Maybe it's the clean mountain air, the abundance of natural pursuits, or the health-minded folks who call Asheville home. Whatever the reason, one thing is true: If you seek to recharge and renew your mind and body, you've come to the right place. Whether you're a beginner or long-practicing yogi, Asheville Wellness Tours provides unique outdoor tours that let you soak in stunning views and immerse yourself in nature. Their two-mile (round trip) yoga hikes lead you to the summit, where you'll begin your session. Sunset hikes are also on offer. Improve your balance and strengthen your core with a SUP yoga class on the French Broad River. Have you ever heard of forest bathing? Inspired by the Japanese practice of immersing yourself in the forest, it's designed to help you pause, restore, and unwind. During this two-and-a-half-hour walk, your guide leads you through a series of invitations to help you focus and reconnect with nature, your community, and yourself.

(828) 407-0711
ashevillewellnesstours.com

PEEP
THE CHANGING MOUNTAIN LEAVES

Each autumn, throngs of leaf peepers from all over make their way to Western North Carolina to view the vibrant display of fall colors. The area lays claim to one of the longest and colorful leaf seasons, thanks to the hundreds of species of deciduous trees and varying elevations. No one can perfectly predict each year's season. The depth of fall color and peak time are determined by environmental factors like weather and elevation. However, peak season generally occurs from late September to early November. Jump on the Blue Ridge Parkway, which runs north to south from Asheville, and take in the scenery from your car. If you don't have a convertible, you might want to rent one! Step out for a crisp fall hike along mile markers 360 to 410. At milepost 364.1, there's a parking overlook and the Craggy Pinnacle Hike. Take a detour onto NC 694 at milepost 377.4 and coast along Town Mountain Road into downtown Asheville. There's also a small parking lot leading to a hike on the Mountains-to-Sea Trail.

EXPLORE ASHEVILLE'S WILD SIDE
AT THE WNC NATURE CENTER

The 42-acre center provides an up-close and personal experience with more than 150 native wildlife of the Southern Appalachian Mountains and endangered species like the American red wolf and red pandas. They offer daily animal programs, behind-the-scenes tours, and even private experiences on habitat with their resident red pandas, Leafa and Phoenix (you get to feed them!). You'll see black bears, foxes, river otters, a cougar, farm animals, and more. This natural heritage site is more than a place to encounter animals. WNC Nature Center is a haven for orphaned, injured, or imprinted animals that cannot survive on their own. It's also one of only 28 facilities in the country participating in the Red Wolf Recovery Program. The center is open every day, year round, and offers a slew of educational and fun events throughout the year.

75 Gashes Creek Rd., (828) 259-8080
wildwnc.org

TIP
Don't miss the wildlife and nature trails! You'll be rewarded with incredible scenic views.

Numerous times over the years,

TAKE A WALK
IN THE WOODS

John Muir once said: "Between every two pines, there is a doorway to a new world." Exploring new worlds is easy to do in Asheville—whether you seek an easy fresh-air stroll or a strenuous workout in the woods. Rattlesnake Lodge Trail offers an easy to moderate hike. It's part of the Mountains-to-Seas Trail, and leads you to the ruins of a 1900s summer lodge. You pass through several switchbacks that follow the old wagon road built to reach the lodge. Craggy Gardens provides a gorgeous high-elevation hike. Encounter thick tunnels of Catawba rhododendron blossoms in middle to late June. A late spring hike yields a bounty of fresh mountain blueberries. You don't need to purchase a ticket to enjoy the trails of the 8,000-acre Biltmore Estate. Varying terrain offers something different along the way—scenic views of the Blue Ridge Mountains, walks along French Broad River, and strolls through the meticulously maintained gardens of the estate.

PLACES TO EXPLORE BEYOND ASHEVILLE

Asheville is the perfect home base for a hiking or mountain biking getaway. The city is ideally situated near hundreds of trails for every activity level. Explore refreshing waterfalls, soak in jaw-dropping summit views, and wind your way through lush forest canopies. Located 40 miles southwest of Asheville, DuPont State Forest offers 10,000 acres of dense forest and granite-domed mountaintops. Fun fact: It's also where *The Hunger Games* was filmed in 2011. Head north from Asheville on the Blue Ridge Parkway to explore Mount Mitchell State Park, the highest point east of the Mississippi River. Asheville is also within an hour of four entrances to the country's most visited national park—the Great Smoky Mountains National Park. Pisgah National Forest spans more than a half million acres across Western North Carolina. It's divided into four districts, with Asheville at the center.

ADMIRE STREET ART
AT FOUNDATION WALLS

In response to the city's attempt to discourage graffiti, property owner Brent Starck decided to take a creative approach in addressing the issue with the Foundation Walls project. Approved by the city in 2016, the project legalized street art on the outside walls of some of the 23 buildings at 339 Lyman Street. Graffiti artists can't just add their work willy-nilly—they're first approved and must follow certain guidelines if they want to participate. They also can't paint over another artist's work unless they know them. If they do cover the original piece, it must be completely covered. The wall's rotating designs span some 13 acres, and are a lure for those seeking to level up their Instagram feed.

339 Old Lyman St.

Visited 07/03/21 after Mrs Bs 95th Bday Party at Harmony. Very neat, talented artists w/ wild imaginations. Needed a partner to help interpret, esp the words, "The Wedge" looked like neat place to get a brew.

PLAY WITH BIRDS OF PREY
AT CURTIS WRIGHT OUTFITTERS

We don't know exactly when the very first person came up with the idea to harness and utilize a bird of prey's natural ability to hunt. However, cave paintings, Chinese pottery, and centuries-old writings indicate the use of falconry. It became the hallmark of wealth and power during the Middle Ages, especially the Stuart monarchs. The ancient art of falconry requires many hours of work and skill. To be able to experience a taste of this "sport of kings" is an incredible encounter. During an hour-and-a-half-long experience, you'll work alongside a licensed falconer and learn the history of this fascinating sport and the different types of birds used in falconry. If you like, you can see what it's like to be a handler, donning a leather glove so the bird can perch on your fist. If you're still shy, you can opt to just observe the technique. Falconry packages are available at the Curtis Wright Outfitters location and at Biltmore Estate (on Thursdays and Saturdays).

24 N Main St., Weaverville, (828) 645-8700
curtiswrightoutfitters.com

Biltmore Estate
Used with permission from The Biltmore Company, Asheville, North Carolina

CULTURE AND HISTORY

BE AWED
BY THE ST. LAWRENCE BASILICA

St. Lawrence Basilica is perhaps one of Asheville's most lavish and detailed architectural features. Designed in 1905 and completed in 1909, it is the final work of Spanish architect and master builder Rafael Guastavino. Although the design and construction of Biltmore Estate was the project that brought him to Asheville, the basilica was perhaps his greatest monument. It's the only basilica in Western North Carolina, and is crowned with one of the country's largest freestanding elliptical domes. The copper dome is guarded by statues of St. Lawrence, St. Aloysius Gonzaga, and St. Stephen. Guastavino used only brick tile, stone, and mortar—no wooden beams or steel in sight. Worship areas feature stained glass windows and wood carvings dating back to the mid-1600s. When Guastavino died in 1908, his son completed construction in 1909. Guastavino rests in the basilica he constructed. You can visit his crypt, located to the left of the main altar. Tours are free, though donations are much appreciated. Choose a guided tour or go it alone. You can grab a brochure in the side vestibule or download a copy from the church website.

08/21/21 w/ Julie. Closed.
Only opened for limited hours on weekdays.

97 Haywood St., (828) 252-6042
saintlawrencebasilica.org

BE INSPIRED
AT BURTON STREET
COMMUNITY PEACE GARDENS

The Burton Street Community Peace Gardens are a beautiful example of how transformative creativity and community can be. In what was once an overgrown and trash-filled lot, flower and vegetable gardens, a greenhouse, and a firepit now welcome visitors. The gardens began thanks to Safi Mahaba and DeWayne Barton who, in 2003, sought to create a peaceful response to the war in Iraq and the scourge of drugs in the United States. The gardens also act as a museum of sorts. Sculptures, found object art, and paintings—many created by Barton—appear around every corner. Volunteers tend the gardens, sharing extra seed starts with neighbors. In addition, the garden helps feed the senior community of the Burton Street neighborhood.

47 Bryant St., (828) 301-0166
urbanpeacegardens.org

STEP BACK IN TIME
AT THE SMITH-MCDOWELL HOUSE MUSEUM

Constructed in 1840 by one of North Carolina's first entrepreneurs, James McConnell Smith, this historic home is Asheville's first mansion and oldest surviving house. (The home predates the construction of Biltmore Estate by 55 years.) It's also Buncombe County's oldest brick structure. Smith was a savvy and influential businessman. Over time, he purchased over 30,000 acres along the French Broad River, which likely contributed to his ability to build such a grand estate during a time when most people lived in modest wood-framed houses. Listed on the National Register of Historic Places, the beautifully restored home serves as a historic museum. Inside the four-story home, tour six period rooms filled with period furnishings for a glimpse at life for the wealthy in antebellum Asheville.

283 Victoria Rd., (828) 253-9231
wnchistory.org-smith-mcdowell-house

HUNT FOR HISTORICAL GRAVESTONES
AT RIVERSIDE CEMETERY

Located in the historic Montford neighborhood, Riverside Cemetery is an ideal place for an easy stroll along paved trails. Designed in 1885 and spanning some 87 acres, it's the final resting place of many notable Asheville citizens. Renowned authors Thomas Wolfe (*Look Homeward, Angel*) and William Sydney Porter, better known as O. Henry (*The Gift of the Magi*) are buried here. Other prominent people here include Isaac Dickson, the first African American appointed to an Asheville City School Board; Quenn Carson, the city's first female public school principal; and James H. Posey, one of Abraham Lincoln's bodyguards.

53 Birch St., (828) 350-2066

TUNE IN
AT THE ASHEVILLE RADIO MUSEUM

Tucked away in a quiet wing of the Asheville-Buncombe Tech Community College, this small museum is a window into the past. A core group of amateur radio operators opened the museum to the public in 2001. Their goal was to educate visitors on the history and importance of radio technology. Prior to the Great Depression, many residents of Western North Carolina lived in remote hollows and on cloistered farms. Telephones were not common, and any news or entertainment beyond their limited area was nonexistent. The popularity of radio in the 1920s changed all that. Farmers had access to broadcasts on weather systems and price reports, allowing them to plan accordingly. Learn about the evolution of radio, as well as get a peek at vintage radios from the 1920s to the 1960s and other historical memorabilia. The museum is open on Saturdays from 1 to 3 p.m. through November. You can also call and schedule your visit. Admission is free.

Asheville-Buncombe Tech Community College
Elm Building, 340 Victoria Rd., Room 315, (504) 256-5796
avlradiomuseum.org

LOOK HOMEWARD
AT THE THOMAS WOLFE MEMORIAL

Get a glimpse of the life of one of America's most prolific writers with a tour of Thomas Wolfe's childhood home. The home "Dixieland" in his classic novel, *Look Homeward, Angel*, was actually his mother's Asheville boardinghouse, "Old Kentucky Home." Wolfe's coming-of-age novel portrays the life and tragedy he experienced growing up there. Upon publication, *Look Homeward, Angel* became an international bestseller. Since its release in 1929, the book has never gone out of print. Knowledgeable and friendly docents lead you through the rambling 29-room home, sharing stories of Wolfe's life, work, and legacy. The museum's visitor center houses some of the author's personal effects, including his Harvard diploma and his Remington typewriter. It's easy to jump in on a tour—they're offered daily and begin at half past each hour (last tour at 4:30 p.m.).

52 N Market St., (828) 253-8304
wolfememorial.com

TIP
Take a side trip to Hendersonville and visit Oakdale Cemetery. You'll find the statue Thomas Wolfe made famous in his iconic novel. In Asheville, visit the bronze statue erected in Wolfe's memory. The wreath-clad angel with a bowed head and outstretched arm is located at 2 South Pack Square.

SEEK OUT
A HIDDEN CASTLE

Built in 1889 by John Evans Brown, Zealandia Castle is situated on Beaucatcher Mountain, overlooking Asheville. The stunning mansion was named for his second home, New Zealand. The architecture was inspired by Moro Castle, located in Havana, Cuba. In 1977, it was added to the list of National Register of Historic Places. Today, it's a venue for many local charity events and galas.

40 Vance Gap Rd.

GET A BIRD'S-EYE VIEW
FROM BILTMORE ESTATE

When you think of Asheville, chances are your first thought is of Biltmore Estate—and it's no wonder. After George Vanderbilt visited the area in 1888, he was so enamored with the climate and scenery, he decided to construct his "little mountain escape" here. His little escape also happens to be the largest private home in America. More than 1.4 million people visited the 8,000-acre estate last year. The palatial home includes 250 rooms, a bowling alley, a 1916 Skinner pipe organ, 16th-century tapestries, triple fireplaces, a two-story library, and troves of other treasures. I've visited Biltmore Estate countless times over the years and never grow tired of it. I always discover something new. One of my favorite tours is the rooftop tour. It gives you such an amazing perspective of the estate grounds and offers awe-inspiring photo ops. You'll discover areas of the home that aren't part of a normal house tour, as well as interesting facts about the home's construction and design. The tour is also limited to six guests, creating a more personalized experience.

One Lodge St., (800) 411-3812
biltmore.com/tour/rooftop-tour

TIP
This tour includes 250 stairs with no elevator access.
Also, strollers and backpacks aren't allowed, so plan accordingly.

STROLL THROUGH HISTORY AND ART
ON THE URBAN TRAIL

This low-key and easy walk is not only the perfect blend of art and history, it gives you a great vantage point to notice all the restaurants, cafes, and bars you might miss driving around in your car. Explore at your own pace on this self-guided walking tour. It showcases the city's art, architecture, and history. The 1.7-mile loop begins and ends in Pack Square. Along the way, you'll stop at 30 points of interest. Among them are Thomas Wolfe's former neighborhood, Grove Arcade, Battery Park Hotel, and several art installations and sculptures. You can find an urban trail map and many downtown locations (the Visitor Center is one), or you can download the map from the Asheville Trails website.

ashevilletrails.com/Asheville/Asheville-urban-trail

Did a lot of this w/ Julie on 08/21/21.
Hard to follow because their map is
poor & inaccurate, but very interesting.
We hit 12 of 30 POIs.

TIP
Build in extra time for your tour, and take breaks at dining spots and bars along the way. You can create your own intermittent food tour!

CHANNEL YOUR INNER NOVELIST
IN THE F. SCOTT FITZGERALD ROOM

The AAA Four Diamond-rated Omni Grove Park Inn has been a getaway for many prominent people for over 107 years. Seriously, their guest list reads like a *Who's Who* of past presidents, historic figures, celebrities, and other notables. F. Scott Fitzgerald is one of those names on the extensive list. Book a room in 441 or 443, where *The Great Gatsby* writer stayed two summers while his wife Zelda was being treated at the psychiatric facility in Asheville's Highland Hospital. He used one room for sleeping, and the other his writing space. The guest rooms were ideally situated above the hotel's bustling courtyard area. He was said to have gleaned writing inspiration from eavesdropping on the conversations that wafted up through his window.

290 Macon Ave., (828) 252-2711
omnihotels.com/hotels/asheville-grove-park

TIP
While you're there, book an indulgent treatment at the subterranean, 43,000-square-foot spa. It's ranked as one of *Condé Nast Traveler's* top resort spas in the country. After your bliss-inducing massage, relax even more in the refreshing contrast pools, saunas, and eucalyptus-infused steam rooms.

08/21/21 w/ Julie.

GET A GLIMPSE
OF ART DECO

Asheville is home to a wealth of Art Deco gems worth noticing. The city boomed in the 1920s, and by 1925, more than 30,000 people called Asheville home. That growth spurred a flurry of construction befitting the metropolis it was becoming. Many of those buildings have been preserved and are still in use, though not necessarily done on purpose. The city suffered terribly from the Great Depression, amassing the highest per capita debt burden of any other US city. The city spent the 50 years following the Depression paying off their debt, leaving no extra money to apply toward redevelopment. Completed in 1927, the Flatiron Building was designed by New York architect Albert Wirth and erected 23 years after the sister building in New York City went up. S.H. Kress and Co. was established by Samuel Henry Kress and operated as a five-and-dime store from 1896 to 1981. Today it's home to Kress Emporium. Completed in 1929, S & W Cafeteria was one of a few Art Deco buildings designed by Douglas Ellington. Also designed by Ellington, Asheville's city hall was completed in 1928. Ellington chose building materials that reflected the natural hues of the area's soil. It was the nation's first Art Deco city hall. Completed in 1924, Jackson Building was constructed on the site where the father of *Look Homeward, Angel* writer Thomas Wolfe operated a monument shop. It's believed that the angel mentioned in the novel was displayed here.

WHERE TO SPOT ART DECO GEMS

Flatiron Building
20 Battery Park Ave.

S.H. Kress & Co.
19 Patton Ave.

S & W Cafeteria
60 Patton Ave.

City Hall
338 Hilliard Ave.

Jackson Building
22 S Pack Square

SINCE 1883

MAST GENERAL STORE

alc

Mast General Store
Photo courtesy of Mast General Store

SHOPPING AND FASHION

WHILE AWAY SOME TIME
AT WHIST

If you need to buy a gift for someone you really, *really* like, this is your spot. You'll find everything from artsy jigsaw puzzles, unique jewelry, and fun canvas totes to distinct greeting cards, colorful journals, and beautiful stationery. They also sell locally made body products and Asheville-centric gifts. The real trick here is to make it out of the store without buying yourself something (or many things).

444 Haywood Rd., #102, (828) 252-5557
whistshop.com

SHUT THE FRONT DOOR FOR HOME DECOR
AT THE SCREEN DOOR

The Screen Door has lured shoppers since 1998. It's a veritable smorgasbord of vintage and antique furnishings, architectural items, art, and accessories. More than 100 vendors occupy the 25,000-square-foot space, providing an eclectic mix of varying decorating styles—antique, modern, industrial, mid-century modern, and country. They also have a huge selection of new and used books—cookbooks, gardening, fashion, and children's books.

115 Fairview Rd., (828) 277-3667
screendoorasheville.com

CORRAL A DEAL
AT THE ANTIQUE TOBACCO BARN

I probably wasn't the only child to have left open a door and heard a cry from my mother: "Were you born in a barn?!" Time spent in the Antique Tobacco Barn makes me wish it were so. With over 75,000 square feet of space, you can spend hours poring over treasures and still crave more time. More than 75 booths almost overflow with furniture, lamps, flatware, and cool tchotchkes. It's easy to see why they're consistently voted as the best place to buy antiques in Western North Carolina. The place is mesmerizing.

75 Swannanoa River Rd., (828) 252-7291
atbarn.com

TIP
If you don't drive a truck or a van, you might want to borrow one before you visit. You don't want to miss out on that perfect table for your dining room because it won't fit in your small trunk.

MAKE A STATEMENT
AT VINTAGE MOON MODERN

Elevate your wardrobe with creatively curated vintage clothing and one-of-a-kind designs from owner Gigi Reneé. Gigi's unique clothing styles mirror nature with earth tones and silhouettes of flowers and leaves. Rummage through racks of lovely dresses, skirts, pants, and shirts to find that signature piece that will garner compliments every time you wear it. In addition to clothing, this charming women's boutique offers jewelry (some locally made), pillows, and home accents.

82 N Lexington Ave., (828) 225-2768
vintagemoonasheville.com

HIT THE BOOKS
AT A BOOKSTORE

Call me old-school, but no electronic device can replicate the joy of cracking open a book, thumbing through its pages, and marking my favorite sections and quotes. No matter where I travel, at some point you'll likely find me perusing bookshelves at the local bookstore. This city feeds my bibliophilia extremely well. The Battery Park Book Exchange & Champagne Bar ticks my list of my two favorite things—books and wine. Sip your rosé while you peruse the shelves, or read your book over a plate of charcuterie, Beauty and the Meats (I kind of love how they name their menu items after well-known books). If you're looking for a rare title, check out Bagatelle Books. They offer a good selection of used books as well. Looking for something specific? Let them know, and they'll be on the lookout for you.

Battery Park Book Exchange & Champagne Bar
1 Page Ave., #101, (828) 252-0020
batteryparkbookexchange.com

Bagatelle Books
428 C Haywood Rd., (828) 774-5585
bagatellebooks.com

TIP
If comics are more your style, Asheville has you covered. Check out Asheville Comics, Morgan's Comics, or Pastimes.

FEEL LIKE CHECKING OUT MORE BOOKSTORES? HERE ARE SOME TO ADD TO YOUR LIST:

Malaprop's Bookstore/Café
55 Haywood St., (828) 254-6734
malaprops.com

Downtown Books & News
67 N Lexington Ave., (828) 253-8654
dbnbooks.com

Firestorm Books & Coffee
610 Haywood Rd., (828) 255-8115
firestorm.coop

FIND IT
AT LOST AND FOUND

Lost and Found Asheville is a cute shop that offers fun, funky retro-inspired clothes with a '50s and '60s flare. Vibrant dresses and skirts with bold designs, cool T-shirts, whimsical handbags, and hair clips—there's a little bit of everything. They also sell the most adorable COVID masks at a reasonable price so you can buy one for each day of the week.

68 College St., (828) 505-3903
facebook.com/lostandfoundavl

SHOP 'TIL YOU DROP
AT THE OUTLETS

When you need a little retail therapy, few places fit the bill like an outlet mall. With a slew of different stores at your credit-card-holding fingertips, you'll feel better in no time. The Asheville Outlets makes it easy, too—park once and shop all day! The mall includes popular retail brands like American Eagle, Banana Republic, Bath & Body Works, Nike, Vineyard Vines, and many more. Break for lunch at Acropolis Pizza Café, then grab yourself a cupcake to go at The Cake Studio before you head home.

800 Brevard Rd.
shopashevilleoutlets.com

GET YOUR HEALTH ON
AT THE HERBIARY

With any bit of time you spend in the Herbiary, it's clear they don't just want to sell you things. They're genuinely interested in helping you improve and nurture your health. Owner Maia Toll apprenticed in Ireland with a traditional healer. The knowledge she gleaned from exploring the growing cycles of plants and the alchemy of medicine making compelled her to open the original Herbiary in Philadelphia. *Forbes* magazine dubbed her a "real-life Professor Sprout from *Harry Potter.*" There's a mind-blowing array of herbs and teas available here, as well as a robust selection of natural remedies, compound tinctures, natural body products, and more. All of their farm-direct herbs are sourced from one of three East Coast herbal farms they have a relationship with and are USDA certified organic.

29 N Market St., (828) 552-3334
herbiary.com

TIP
If you're interested in learning more about the healing attributes of herbs, check out Maia's book, *The Illustrated Herbiary*. She also runs a blog at MaiaToll.com.

FIND
THE PERFECT VINYL

The old-school way of listening to music has made a steady comeback over the past years. As of 2019, vinyl album sales in the United States have grown for the 14th consecutive year. Whether you're new to the LP scene or you want to restock your original collection that made its way to a yard sale at some point in the mid-'90s, you have some options in Asheville. Harvest Records has been around since 2004, and they've curated a huge inventory of vinyl records, CDs, cassettes, and DVDs. They also sell books, stereo equipment, and vinyl accessories. Voltage Records sells lots of different styles of music—rock, soul, alternative, and others. Static Age Records offers a good variety of vinyl records as well.

Harvest Records
415 Haywood Dr., (828) 258-2999
harvest-records.com

Voltage Records
90 N Lexington Ave., (828) 255-9333
facebook.com/voltageavl

Static Age Records
110 N Lexington Ave., (828) 254-3232
facebook.com/static.agerecords.7

SECURE A LOCAL SOUVENIR
AT MOUNTAIN MERCH

A visitor seeking a wide range of Asheville-inspired souvenirs will hit the jackpot here. And we're not talking shot glasses, tacky T-shirts, and poorly painted snow globes, either. The gifts you find at Mountain Merch are the kinds you buy two of—one for your friend and one for yourself. In addition to the community-centric clothing and hats on offer, they sell thoughtfully selected products from local makers. Shop leather bags and wood items from InBlue, shampoo from BRÖÖ, body products from Essential Journeys, and pottery from Muddy Llama.

22 Lodge St., (828) 708-7802
mtnmerch.com

GET HIPPY DIPPY
AT INSTANT KARMA

For me, Instant Karma seems to embody the true essence of Asheville. The atmosphere is fun, free-spirited, and unique. The shop has been helping locals and visitors stay groovy for more than 20 years. Stock up on tie-dye apparel, essential oils, incense, CBD items, locally made bath products, Baja hoodies, patches, and enough Grateful Dead and Jerry Garcia items to please even the most devoted Deadhead.

36 N Lexington Ave., (828) 301-8187
725 Waywood Rd., (828) 285-8999
instantkarmaasheville.com

APPRECIATE HERITAGE ARTS
AT THE APPALACHIAN CRAFT CENTER

Created in 1980, the Appalachian Craft Center was designed to support Appalachian potters by providing them a place to display and market their works. Since then, it has grown to showcase all types of talent that abounds in North Carolina and the Southern Appalachians. More than 150 artists skilled in traditional folk art are represented. The center features a distinct selection of handcrafted pottery and face jugs, as well as etchings, prints, handmade rugs, and wood crafts. If you like to wear your art, choose from a variety of unique handcrafted bracelets, necklaces, and earrings. Make sure to grab a jar or two of locally made jams, jellies, or honey.

10 N Spruce St., Ste. 120, (828) 253-8499

BE IMPRESSED
WITH KRESS EMPORIUM

The gorgeous Art Deco-style building is enough to lure you in. The 1926 Kress Building landed on the National Register of Historic Places in 1979. Once you enter, you're flooded with a beautiful palette of color and textures created from more than 100 local and regional artists. You'll also find antiques, collectibles, photography, and plants. There's a good bit of room to walk around, and the vendor booths are well-organized. Head downstairs to browse their selection of furniture. When you finish shopping, visit their sister store located just two doors down.

19 Patton Ave., (828) 281-2252
27 Patton Ave., (828) 232-7237
thekressemporium.com

BUZZ AROUND
ASHEVILLE BEE CHARMER

When owners Jillian Kelly and Kim Allen decided to reduce their consumption of refined sugar, they used raw honey to replace it. This small change sparked a desire to learn more about bees and other pollinators. Kelly and Allen moved from their Chicago home to Asheville to pursue their interest in earnest, and Asheville Bee Charmer was born. If you don't know much about honey and how we get it, this is the perfect place to learn. They have more than 50 varieties of honey here. Staff members are patient and knowledgeable, and will help you find the perfect jar (or jars) for you. You can't go wrong with the sourwood honey, made in North Carolina. Or, go for an infused honey with a hint of hot peppers, chai, cocoa, or lavender. You'll also find a good selection of honey-related products like spreads, lotions, soaps, home items, and gift sets.

38 Battery Park Ave., (828) 424-7274
32 Broadway, (828) 505-7736
ashevillebeecharmer.com

08/21/21 w/ Julie.

BUY YOUR BASICS AND MORE
AT MAST GENERAL STORE

A visit to Mast General Store is like stepping back to a simpler time. It's situated in an 1846 building that served many businesses back in the day, including Fain's Thrift Store (in 1946). The charm of the building's history is hard to resist. You can even see the original terrazzo inlaid tile from Fain's in the front part of the store. Mast General Store is a cornucopia of all mountain town essentials and much more. I'm inclined to believe if you can't find what you're looking for at Mast General Store, it doesn't exist. The store has books, body care products, an extensive selection of outdoor gear and clothing from well-established brands, toys, and countless other things you didn't realize you needed. Pick up a jar of Mast Store Provisioners apple butter, jams, or moonshine jelly. Perusing the barrels of colorful candy is always a treat for me. Stuff your bag with a variety of your favorite sweets—chocolate bars, old-fashioned sugar stick candy, gum, rock candy, and more.

15 Biltmore Ave., (828) 232-1883
mastgeneralstore.com/asheville

SPICE THINGS UP
AT THE PEPPER PALACE

This family-owned business began in 1989 in a Wisconsin mall. The demand for heat grew quickly, and their small business evolved into a group of more than 80 locations in the US and Canada. Their growth didn't compromise their process, though. The homemade sauces are still produced in small batches. Their award-winning sauces come in several levels of heat tolerance. If you're not into hot sauce, try their salsas, seasonings, pepper jellies, drink mixes, and a bevy of other spicy creations.

6 College St., Unit 6, (828) 424-7152
pepperpalace.com/pages/asheville-nc

GET THRIFTY
AND SHOP SECONDHAND

Few things are more fun to me than scoping out thrift stores for a great bargain on a *Golden Girls*-inspired silk jacket or a purse that resembles one my mother carried in the '70s. Mismatched coffee mugs, a Sonny and Cher album, vintage Christmas decorations—you never know what treasure is right around the corner. Whether you're looking for gently used clothing that's "new" to you or wanting to add pieces to your living room gallery wall, there are so many options!

Second Chances Thrift Store
49 Glendale Ave., (828) 505-2017
bwar.org/second-chances-thrift-store

Etc. Consignment Shoppe
1500 Patton Ave., (828) 251-1160
etcconsignmentshoppeasheville.com

Estate Sale Services and Thrift Store
75 Fairview Rd., (828) 274-8206
wncbridge.org/shop/thrift-store

Enchanted Forrest
(women's apparel and accessories)
235 Merrimon Ave., (828) 236-0688
enchantedforrestasheville.com

Clothes Mentor
1829 Hendersonville Rd., #100,
(828) 274-4901
clothesmentor.com/asheville

The Regeneration Station
26 Glendale Ave., B, (828) 505-1108
regenerationstation.com

Reciprocity
732 Haywood Rd., (828) 505-3980
reciprocityasheville.com

Second Gear
444 Haywood Rd., (828) 258-0757
secondgearwnc.com

TIP
Did you find something amazing during your visit? Share your Asheville thrifting finds with me on Instagram! Use #100ThingsAsheville.

SUGGESTED
ITINERARIES

ART LOVERS

Get Your Art Fix at Museums and Galleries, 50

Admire Street Art at Foundation Walls, 100

Hit the Trail for Urban Art, 48

Appreciate Heritage Arts at the Appalachian Craft Center, 130

Go with the Flow in the River Arts District, 57

ROMANTIC GETAWAY

Lay Down a Track at American Vinyl Co., 59

Enjoy Late-Night Date-Night Sweets with Your Sweet
    at Old Europe Pastries, 12

Stay in a Gem, and Sleep Like a King, 90

Stay Up Late for Nightlife, 72

GIRLS' WEEKEND

Rub Elbows with James Beard Royalty, 28

Sample a Flight at Plēb Urban Winery, 10

Find Your Center in the Mountains, 95

Zoom Around the City in a Purple Bus, 69

Get Salty at the Asheville Salt Cave, 80

• •

HISTORY BUFFS

Be a Pinball Wizard at the Asheville Pinball Museum, 78

Sip a Shake at the Soda Fountain at Woolworth Walk, 30

Step Back in Time at the Smith-McDowell House Museum, 106

Rove Around Historic Grove Arcade, 66

BOOK LOVERS

Channel Your Inner Novelist in the F. Scott Fitzgerald Room, 113

Hit the Books at a Bookstore, 122

Look Homeward at the Thomas Wolfe Memorial, 109

FAMILY FUN

Hop on the Gray Line Trolley, 62

Eat Like a Food Show Host, 18

Pop In for a Pie at Baked Pie Company, 34

Play with Birds of Prey at Curtis Wright Outfitters, 101

Get Lost in Nature at the N.C. Arboretum, 92

OUTDOOR EXPLORERS

Float Down the French Broad, 83

Don't Stop Your Bellyaking, 79

Amp Up Your Camping with Asheville Glamping, 89

Search for Your Supper with No Taste Like Home, 13

Take a Walk in the Woods, 98

● ●

FOR THE FOODIES

Eat BBQ and Take a Selfie at 12 Bones Smokehouse, 26

Nosh Through Asheville on a Food Tour, 4

Toast to Asheville's First Brewery at Highland Brewing, 24

Visit Cuba Without a Passport at Hemingway's Cuba, 15

Buzz Around Asheville Bee Charmer, 132

SHOP AROUND

Get Hippy Dippy at Instant Karma, 129

Corral a Deal at the Antique Tobacco Barn, 120

Secure a Local Souvenir at Mountain Merch, 128

Get Your Health On at the Herbiary, 126

ANIMAL LOVERS

Talk to the Animals at Animal Haven of Asheville, 82

Explore Asheville's Wild Side at the WNC Nature Center, 97

Go Vegan for a Meal (or Three!), 38

Go to the Dogs, 86

• •

ACTIVITIES
BY SEASON

SPRING

Track Down Food Trucks on the Go, 21

Explore Historic Grovewood Village, 51

Catch a Show at Grey Eagle Music Hall, 58

Cheer on Runners at the Asheville Marathon, 76

Tee Off with a Round of Golf, 85

SUMMER

Float Down the French Broad, 83

Feast on Local Fare (and More) at a Farmers Market, 31

Soak in the Busking Scene, 52

Take Yourself Out to the Ballgame at McCormick Field, 77

Pack a Picnic Spot and Graze, 42

Take a Walk in the Woods, 98

FALL

Meet a Motley Fool with Montford Park Players, 60

Hunt for Historical Gravestones at Riverside Cemetery, 107

Chow Down at Chow Chow: An Asheville Culinary Event, 2

- -

Get Spooked on a Ghost Tour with Haunted Asheville, 84

Walk Along Wall Street, 64

Peep the Changing Mountain Leaves, 96

WINTER

Get Your Art Fix at Museums and Galleries, 50

Have a Tea Party at the Inn on Biltmore Estate, 7

Ring In the Holidays at the Omni Grove Park Inn National Gingerbread House Competition, 63

Cure What Ails You at Sovereign Remedies, 6

INDEX

12 Bones, 18–19, 26, 138

1889 WhiteGate Inn & Cottage, 90–91

1900 Inn on Montford, 90–91

Abbington Green Bed & Breakfast Inn and Spa, 90–91

Albemarle Inn, 90–91

Aloft Asheville Downtown, 86–87

American Vinyl Co., 59, 136

Amy's Bakery, 35

Animal Haven of Asheville, 82, 138

Antique Tobacco Barn, 120, 138

Appalachian Chic Food Truck, 21

Appalachian Craft Center, 50, 130, 136

Archetype Brewing, 86–87

Asheville Art Museum, 50

Asheville Bee Charmer, 132, 138

Asheville Brewing Company, 25

Asheville Distilling Co., 23

Asheville Emporium, 64–65

Asheville Food Tours, 4–5

Asheville Food Trucks, 21

Asheville Fringe Arts Festival, 53

Asheville Glamping, 89, 137

Asheville Marathon, 76, 139

Asheville Municipal Golf Course, 85

Asheville Museum of Science, 73

Asheville Outdoor Center, 83

Asheville Outlets, 125

Asheville Pinball Museum, 78, 137

Asheville Radio Museum, 108

Asheville Rooftop Tours, 14

Asheville Salt Cave, 80

Asheville Sandwich Co., 18–19, 42

Asheville Urban Trail, 64, 112

Asheville VeganFest, 3

Asheville Wellness Tours, 95

Asheville Wine Market, 11

Azalea Dog Park, 86–87

Bagatelle Books, 122

Baked Pie Company, 34, 137

Battery Park Book Exchange & Champagne Bar, 66, 122

Beer City Week, 3

Bellyak, 79, 137

Benne on Eagle, 28–29

Biltmore Estate, 7, 43, 55, 76, 83, 90–91, 98, 101, 104, 106, 111, 140

Biltmore Estate Winery, 11

Biltmore Village Inn, 90–91

BimBeriBon, 18–19

Biscuit Head, 18–19

Black Bear BBQ, 27

Blackbird, The, 18–19

Black Mountain College Museum and Art Center, 50

Black Walnut Bed & Breakfast Inn, The, 86–87

Blomkraft Studio, 64–65

Blue Ridge Parkway, The, 43, 56, 96, 99

Bonfire BBQ & Catering, 27

Botanical Gardens at Asheville, 43, 94

Burial Beer Co., 25, 49

Burton Street Community Peace Gardens, 105

Buxton Hall Barbecue, 27–29

Carolina Mountain Cheese Fest, 3

Carolina Small Batch Beer Festival, 3

Chai Pani, 18–19, 28–29

Chemist, The, 22

Chow Chow: An Asheville Culinary Event, 2

City Hall, 114–115

Clothes Mentor, 135

Cottage Cooking Asheville, 9

Craggy Gardens, 43, 98

Cucina 24, 18–19, 28–29, 64–65

Cultivated Cocktails Distillery, 23

Curaté, 28–29

Curtis Wright Outfitters, 101, 137

Dalton Distillery, 22

Dickey's Barbecue Pit, 27

Dog City, U.S.A., 65, 87

Dolce Vita, 64–65

Double D's Coffee & Desserts, 36

Downtown Books & News, 123

DuPont State Forest, 55, 99

Early Girl Eatery, 18–19, 41, 64–65

East Asheville Tailgate Market, 33

Eating Asheville, 4–5

Eda Rhyne Distilling Company, 23

Empyrean Arts, 71

Enchanted Forrest, 135

Estate Sale Services and Thrift Store, 135

Etc. Consignment Shoppe, 135

Eurisko Beer Company, 86–87

Farm Burger, 8

Firestorm Books & Coffee, 123

Fitzgerald, F. Scott, 113, 137

Flatiron Building, the, 114–115

Folk Art Center, The, 56

Foundation Walls Project, The, 100

French Broad Chocolate Lounge, 2, 16

French Broad Outfitters, 83

French Broad River Brewery, 86–87

French Broad River Dog Park, 86–87

Geraldine's, 35

Grand Bohemian Hotel Asheville, 90–91

Great Smoky Mountains National Park, 99

Green Man Brewery, 25

Green Sage Café, 41

Grey Eagle Music Hall, 58, 139

Grove Arcade, 52, 66, 112, 137

Grovewood Village, 51, 139

Harvest Records, 127

Haunted Asheville, 84, 140

Helen's Bridge, 88

Hemingway's Cuba, 15, 138

Herbiary, The, 126, 138

Highland Brewing, 24–25, 138

Hilton Asheville Biltmore Park, 90–91

Historic Gray Line Asheville Trolley Tours, 86–87

Hola Asheville Festival, 3

Inn on Biltmore Estate, The, 7, 90–91, 140

Instant Karma, 129, 138

Jackson Building, 114, 115

Jerusalem Garden Café, 17

Karen Donatelli Bakery & Café, 35

Kress Emporium, 114, 131

La Bodega by Curaté, 28–29
Lake Powhatan Recreation Area, 43, 92
Laughing Seed Café, 38, 64–65
LaZoom Tours, 69
Lexington Glassworks, 68
Lion & Rose Bed and Breakfast, 37
Little Pigs BBQ, 27
Little Switzerland Orchard
    and Winery, 11
Lost and Found Asheville, 124
Luella's Bar-B-Que, 18–19, 27
Malaprop's Bookstore, 123
Market Place, 64–65
Mast General Store, 116, 133
McCormick Field, 77, 139
Melt Your Heart Food Truck, 21
Metro Wines, 11
Moe's Original BBQ, 27
Montford Park Players, 60–61, 139
Moog Music, 47
Moogseum, 47
Moose Café, 18–19
Mountain Merch, 128, 138
Mount Mitchell State Park, 99
Mural Trail, The, 48–49
Nantahala Outdoor Center, 83
N.C. Arboretum, 92, 137
Nine Mile Asheville, 20
North Asheville Tailgate Market, 32
No Taste Like Home Tours, 13, 137
O. Henry's, 72
Old Europe Pastries, 12, 136
Old World Levain Bakery
    (OWL Bakery), 35

Omni Grove Park Inn, The, 63, 85–87,
    90–91, 113, 140
Patton Avenue Pet Company West, 64,
    73, 86–87
Paul Taylor Sandals, 64–65
Pepper Palace, The, 134
Pisgah National Forest, 92, 99
Plant, 38
Plēb Urban Winery, 10, 32
Public Drum Circle, 54
Rankin Vault Cocktail Lounge, 72
Reciprocity, 35
Regeneration Station, The, 135
Rhu, The, 42
Rhubarb, 18–19, 28–29
River Arts District, The, 32, 49, 57,
    83, 136
River Arts District Farmers Market, 32
Riverside Cemetery, 107, 139
Rocky's Hot Chicken Shack, 18–19
Roman's Deli & Catering, 42
Root Down food truck, 21
Rosetta's Kitchen, 40
S.H. Kress & Co., 114–115
S & W Cafeteria, 114–115
Screen Door, 119
Second Chances Thrift Store, 135
Second Gear, 135
Shortie's Drive-Thru BBQ, 27
Silver River Chairs, 70
Smith-McDowell House Museum,
    106, 137
Southern Highland Craft Guild, 56
Sovereign Remedies, 6, 140
Spring Herb Festival, 3

● ●

Static Age Records, 127

St. Lawrence Basilica, 104

Sunflower Diner, 40

Table, 28–29

Taste Carolina, 4–5

Thirsty Monk Brewery, 25

Thomas Wolfe Memorial, The, 109, 137

Trade and Lore Coffee, 64–65

Vintage Moon Modern, 121

Visitor Center, 46, 94

Voltage Records, 127

Vortex Doughnuts, 40

WNC Farmers Market, 31–32

Well Played Board Game Café, 64–65

West Asheville Tailgate Market, 20, 33

Whist, 118

WNC Nature Center, 97

Woolworth Walk, 30, 52, 137

Zealandia Castle, 110

Zealandia Mansion, 88